The ISO/TS 16949
Implementation Guide

Most Paton Press books are available at quantity discounts when purchased in bulk. For more information, contact:

Paton Press LLC
PO Box 44
Chico, CA 95927-0044
Telephone: (530) 342-5480
Fax: (530) 342-5471
E-mail: *books@patonpress.com*
Web: *www.patonpress.com*

10 09 08 07 06 05 04   10 9 8 7 6 5 4 3 2 1

ISBN 1-932828-01-X

Staff

Publisher ....Scott M. Paton
Editor ....Finn Kraemer
Book Design ....Caylen Balmain

Contents

About the Author and Contributors

Chad Kymal is an international trainer and consultant whose broad experience includes TQM, setup reduction, technology assessment and inventory analysis, statistical process control, and quality function deployment. He was on the Malcolm Baldrige Board of Examiners and is an RAB-certified lead auditor. He has a bachelor's degree in mechanical engineering from General Motors Institute, a master's degree in industrial and operations engineering from the University of Michigan, and an MBA from the University of Michigan.

Kymal founded Omnex Inc., a business/quality management solution provider to semiconductor, automotive, manufacturing, and service industries. He led the Omnex team that helped Ford Motor Co. rewrite the QOS methodology. He helped write the QS-9000 requirements and did the first worldwide witness audit for the same. Omnex has worked with Lucent Technologies, Philips Semiconductors, Magna, and most of the Fortune 500 companies worldwide. Omnex provides more than 50 training courses in subject areas ranging from APQP to Six Sigma and has 15 offices worldwide.

Kymal is also the founder of AQSR, one of the top five rated quality system registrars in the United States as rated by *Quality Digest*. AQSR specializes in providing auditing services in ISO 9001, QS-9000, TE Supplement, ISO/TS 16949, VDA 6*, AS9000, and the ISO 14001 series of international standards.

Kymal also founded Omnex Systems, which provides Omnex's industry-leading Advance Product Quality Planning Software, AQuA®. Currently, Omnex Systems is offering the Enterprise-wide Quality Management System (EwQMS™) Suite, which features AQuA Pro, Audit Pro, Boss, Document Pro, MSA Pro, HR Pro, Process Analyzer, Process Pro, and TPM Pro.

Kymal worked closely with the Automotive Electronic Council (AEC) to develop the Semiconductor Supplement and was named executive director of the Semiconductor Assembly Council (SAC). He is currently leading SAC in the development of a second-party/third-party auditing process for the semiconductor supply chain. He is also helping SAC remove waste and redundancy in quality system requirements auditing in the semiconductor supply chain.

Dave Watkins is executive vice president and director of international operations for Omnex. He has a wide range of experience encompassing full profit and loss responsibility in manufacturing, production, and distribution management in custom molded thermosets and thermosetting materials, chemical processing, metal fabrication and synthetic fibers.

Watkins' focus is on enhancing the clients' ability to create value for customers and stockholders through integrated approaches to QOS/BOS, ISO 9001/QS-9000, and new product development and launch (APQP). He is particularly adept at the integration of quality and management systems to enhance performance.

Watkins has authored or co-authored most of Omnex's service classes, including ISO 9000 for QSA-S, AQP for Service, and QOS for Service as well as leading the team that developed Omnex's highly regarded APQP Implementation and Improvement training. He has trained most of Ford's STAs (both service and manufacturing) in ISO 9001, QOS and APQP.

Watkins' education includes a bachelor's degree from Widener University and numerous professional courses. He has served on the board of directors of the Illinois Manufacturers' Association, as a trustee for the IMA's Education Foundation, and as a trustee for Northeastern Illinois University Foundation.

Andy Cheek is vice president of operations for AQSR International. He leads the automotive certification schemes for AQSR International and is the AQSR corporate representative for ISO/TS 16949:2002. He has 12 years' experience working worldwide in third-party certification in various manufacturing industries, predominantly the automotive industry. Auditor certifications are held for ISO 9001:2000, QS-9000, QS-9000 Tooling & Equipment, VDA 6.1, ISO/TS 16949:1999, and ISO/TS 16949:2002.

Prior to working for AQSR he was the automotive technology manager for one of the world's largest registrars responsible for the automotive schemes and the training and development of auditors. Cheek has designed and delivered various presentations regarding third-party certification schemes both to internal staff and clients worldwide.

Prior to working in the third-party certification industry, he was a quality manager for a transmission plant in the United Kingdom. His academic qualifications are in industrial engineering and industrial/operations management.

Preface

W. Edwards Deming, Joseph M. Juran, Philip Crosby, and Kaoru Ishikawa are probably the four most influential persons behind the quality movement. Each of these personalities has left an indelible mark on U.S. automotive quality requirements. In turn, many of the strategies used by U.S. automakers have influenced a significant number of other industries worldwide—from electronics to textiles, from steel to plastics to semiconductors, just to name a few.

The U.S. automakers' strategy of requiring their first-tier suppliers to meet quality requirements is unprecedented in the history of any industry. The purchasing strength of the automobile industry, although fast waning due to market share loss, is what allows this domination and influence. This approach was also fueled by Deming's dictum to both work with and simultaneously reduce the supplier base to improve industry performance. Working with suppliers and the effects of suppliers is certainly even more important in this decade. At this juncture, when services are being outsourced to India and manufacturing is being outsourced to China, the departure from ISO/TS 16949 (unlike QS-9000) as a supply chain standard is indeed surprising (see chapter 5).

When the predecessors of ISO/TS 16949 were initiated twenty-five years ago, quality was recognized as a major determinant of costs, and the industry understood the concepts of the "hidden factory" (Crosby) and the need to present quality costs to top management in terms of dollars (Juran and Crosby). Due to significant reductions in product PPMs, traditional methods for calculating cost of quality have diminished in significance. It's now difficult for quality professionals or top management to explain why implementing these standards is relevant to their organization. Ironically, at this moment automotive organizations are working hard to reduce costs and improve design through a number of programs and initiatives. In this climate, ISO/TS 16949 has the potential to be great.

It's up to quality professionals to implement ISO/TS 16949, or other quality initiatives, so that top management sees the relevance of such work. Chapters 1 through 10 discuss how ISO/TS 16949:2002 should be implemented to provide the most value to organizations.

The next twenty years are going to be the most challenging years for automotive OEMs and their suppliers worldwide. New automakers will enter the fray. We are told that Toyota is no longer looking at Ford, GM, or DaimlerChrysler but at the low costs and high quality of Hyundai. The Big Three have a right to be concerned: Tata, the Indian maker of the Indica, has set a goal of making a car for $2,000. New suppliers from China and India will enter the supplier market with ISO/TS 16949 certification and with costs at half of what most automotive suppliers in the low technology end incur. Of course, they will acquire the low technology end and slowly move into high-technology parts, because research and development and intellectual capital are cheap in their countries. Outsourcing, while defending the low end, coupled with a commitment to supply a wide variety of OEMs, will be key to top management strategy.

Consistently satisfying customer expectations (the basis for determining strategy and objectives), improvement of processes worldwide, and measurement and overall improvement in a number of strategic areas are critical to the survival of the automobile industry. Not coincidentally, all of these issues happen to be critical ISO/TS 16949:2002 factors.

Many large tier-one suppliers are doing well now and have earned grades ranging from an A- to a B+. However, they share the same fate many OEMs will face in the next twenty-five years as the supplier playing field becomes much more competitive.

Other key concepts being neglected include the management of key indicators from multiple operations worldwide, the management and integration of product and process design, and a particularly key value of the system—knowledge management. In addition, the value of information technology in fulfilling and integrating these operations cannot be overstated.

In summary, the key message from this book is the need for acquiring value from ISO/TS 16949 implementation. Either directly or indirectly, ISO/TS 16949 will have an effect on the key movements in the automobile industry in this decade, namely:

- Outsourcing of manufacturing and services to China and India and the need for strong systems for supplier development and monitoring
- The need for the implementation of standards and management systems to be relevant to top management issues of cost reduction, lead time reduction, speed in new product design and development with first pass success, and the resulting healthy financial performance
- The importance of customer expectations and requirements driving strategy, objectives, processes, measurement, and improvement in a company operating with management and factories worldwide and dependent upon a global supply chain
- The importance of implementing an enterprisewide quality management software system

I hope you enjoy this book. Please feel free to e-mail me directly with your comments. As this book goes to press, I will be busy working on my next book on auditing ISO/TS 16949.

—*Chad Kymal*

ckymal@omnex.com

Chapter 1

History of Automotive Quality Requirements

The 1980s were challenging years in the automotive industry. General Motors had more than 39 percent of the market share, while Ford had 22 percent, and Chrysler had 11 percent. In 1986, imports had taken 27.6 percent of the market share, and the forecast was that their market share might go even higher in the 1990s. Alarm bells were going off in Detroit.

Quality was the talk of the day, and Japanese quality was under particular scrutiny. Quality circles, design of experiments, and upfront quality were subjects of special interest. (For a detailed look at the history of quality-related methodologies and movements in the U.S. automotive industry, see figure 1.1.)

Key influences in the automotive industry were W. Edwards Deming and Joseph M. Juran. Each individual has left an indelible imprint on automotive industry standards and methodologies. What we owe to these two giants can't adequately be discussed in this book; however, we would be remiss if we didn't include Deming's 14 Points for Management (see figure 1.2).

A PROLIFERATION OF REQUIREMENTS

The 1980s also spawned the advent of three North American automotive OEM quality requirements: Ford's Q-101 Guidelines, GM's Target for Excellence, and Chrysler's Supplier Quality Guidelines. In addition to these, many first-tier suppliers to automotive OEMs issued their own quality requirements. For example, Johnson Controls, Bosch, and TRW each developed quality requirements for their suppliers. Suppliers of commodities such as steel were audited with a different quality requirement almost every other day. These multiple requirements often referred to the same topic with different names or used similar names for different topics.

Figure 1.1—Movement of Methodologies and Thought in the U.S. Automotive Industry

Era	Focus
1980s	■ Statistical process control ■ Control plans and failure mode and effects diagrams ■ Initial sample report ■ Gage repeatability and reproducibility ■ Disciplined problem solving (8-D) ■ Supplier programs and supplier reduction ■ Elimination of receiving inspection
1990s	■ Lean manufacturing ■ Quality operating system (QOS) ■ Mistake-proofing
2000s	■ Six Sigma ■ Lean Six Sigma ■ Enterprise quality management software ■ Second-tier supplier programs

In 2004, U.S. automotive programs continue to focus on Lean, Six Sigma, integrated software systems, mistake-proofing, and second-tier supplier programs.

Many felt this proliferation of requirements was nonvalue adding. The Detroit chapter of the American Society for Quality was concerned about this situation and approached the vice presidents of Ford, GM, and Chrysler about the problem.

In response, the automotive OEMs created the Automotive Industry Action Group (AIAG), a nonprofit association that allowed a controlled, open discussion of quality requirements. They also formed the Automotive Task Force (ATF) to work on the harmonization of quality requirements. This team developed the *Failure Mode and Effects Analysis* (FMEA), *Statistical Process Control* (SPC), *Measurement Systems Analysis* (MSA), *Advanced Product Quality Planning* (APQP), and *Production Part Approval Process* (PPAP) manuals. They also worked on harmonizing the automotive OEMs' quality system requirements.

Figure 1.2—W. Edwards Deming's 14 Points for Management

- Create a constancy of purpose
- Adopt the new philosophy
- Cease dependence on mass inspection
- End the practice of awarding business on the basis of price tag alone
- Improve constantly and forever the system of production and services
- Institute training
- Adopt and institute leadership
- Drive out fear
- Break down barriers between departments
- Eliminate slogans, exhortations, and targets for the work force
- Eliminate numerical quotas for the work force
- Remove barriers that rob people of pride of workmanship
- Institute a vigorous program of education and self-improvement
- Put everyone in the organization to work to accomplish the transformation.

QS-9000

The result of the ATF's harmonization efforts was QS-9000, which was released in 1994 as a reaction to the proliferation of quality requirements in the automotive industry. This marked the first time that the entire North American automotive industry had adopted a single quality system requirement. The effect of QS-9000 was also felt internationally—as far away as China and as close as Mexico. By 2001, more than 22,500 companies were registered to QS-9000, through 174 registrars and twenty-two accreditation bodies.

The ATF built QS-9000 around the International Organization for Standardization's (ISO) quality management system standard, known as ISO 9001:1994. Each OEM worked on merging its quality system requirements to ISO 9001:1994. Although some automotive requirements were added by the OEMs as "shalls" (i.e., mandatory requirements), others were added as "shoulds" (i.e., mandatory requirements with some flexibility).

ISO 9001:1994 and QS-9000 can be compared by counting the difference in the number of "shalls" and "shoulds" in the text of each. Table 1.1 shows the comparison between ISO 9001:1994 and QS-9000, Third Edition.

Table 1.1—Comparison of "Shalls" and "Shoulds" in ISO 9001:1994 and QS-9000

Element	ISO Shall	QS-9000 Shall	QS-9000 Should
4.1	9	22	8
4.2	9	37	13
4.3	5	6	1
4.4	20	37	2
4.5	9	10	1
4.6	11	17	4
4.7	2	3	0
4.8	3	3	0
4.9	7	27	5
4.10	16	32	4
4.11	16	14	3
4.12	2	3	0
4.13	7	17	1
4.14	5	12	0
4.15	9	23	0
4.16	7	12	0
4.17	6	6	2
4.18	3	4	1
4.19	1	2	0
4.20	2	3	2
Total	149	290	47

QS-9000 has 150 percent more "shalls" and "shoulds" than ISO 9001:1994. QS-9000 and ISO 9001:1994 are primarily manufacturing-based, with nine of the twenty requirements focused on plants. QS-9000 is more business-focused than ISO 9001:1994, and it has additional requirements for business planning, design (APQP), supplier development, continual improvement, and customer satisfaction. (For more on ISO and ISO 9000, see table 1.2.)

Table 1.2—ISO and ISO 9000

About ISO	About ISO 9001:2000
ISO is a network of the national standards institutes of 147 countries, on the basis of one member per country, with a Central Secretariat in Geneva, Switzerland, that coordinates the system.	ISO 9001:2000 specifies requirements for a quality management system for any organization that needs to demonstrate its ability to consistently provide products that meet customer and applicable regulatory requirements and aims to enhance customer satisfaction.
ISO is a nongovernmental organization: Its members are not, as is the case in the United Nations system, delegations of national governments. Nevertheless, ISO occupies a special position between the public and private sectors. This is because, on one hand, many of its member institutes are part of the governmental structure of their countries or are mandated by their government. On the other hand, other members have their roots uniquely in the private sector, having been set up by national partnerships of industry associations.	ISO 9001:2000 is used in seeking to establish a management system that provides confidence in the conformance of your product to established or specified requirements. It is now the only standard in the ISO 9000 family against whose requirements a quality system can be certified by an external agency. The standard recognizes that the word "product" applies to services, processed material, hardware, and software intended for, or required by, your customer.
Therefore, ISO is able to act as a bridging organization in which a consensus can be reached on solutions that meet both the requirements of business and the broader needs of society, such as the needs of stakeholder groups like consumers and users.	There are five sections in the standard that specify activities that need to be considered when implementing a system. You must describe the activities you use to supply your products and may exclude the parts of the product realization section that are not applicable to your operations. The requirements in the other four sections—quality management system; management responsibility; resource management; and measurement,
What ISO's Name Means Because "International Organization for Standardization" would have different	

abbreviations in different languages ("IOS" in English, "OIN" in French for Organisation Internationale de Normalisation), it was decided at the outset to use a word derived from the Greek *isos,* meaning "equal."

Therefore, whatever the country, whatever the language, the short form of the organization's name is always ISO.

analysis, and improvement—apply to all organizations, and you must demonstrate how you apply them to your organization in your quality manual or other documentation.

VDA 6.1

In countries where German automakers have a strong market share, there were two competing requirements—QS-9000 and VDA 6.1. For example, in Brazil, Mexico, and China, automotive suppliers were asked to adopt both QS-9000 and VDA 6.1. (For more on VDA and VDA 6.1, see table 1.3.) This resulted in dual system requirements and audits. This fact, coupled with the merger of Chrysler and Daimler-Benz in 1998, resulted in U.S. automakers inviting Europeans to work with them to develop a harmonized European-American automotive requirement.

In 1998, this objective was nearly achieved, but a final agreement between the U.S. OEMs (QS-9000) and the European OEMs (EAQF, AVSQ, and VDA) was not reached. The ATF decided to release a third edition of QS-9000. Many automotive industry observers had expected the third edition to be a harmonized set of U.S. and European quality system requirements. However, the third edition only had an acceptance that either the U.S. or European requirements could be used for internal auditing and supplier development.

ISO/TS 16949:1999

The U.S. and European automakers continued to work together, and in 1999 they were ready to release a harmonized set of U.S. and European requirements. One of the techniques that they used to find common ground was the removal of any requirement that they both could not agree to. QS-9000 requirements missing in ISO/TS 16949:2002 didn't disappear but became customer-specific requirements for the U.S. automakers. The joint task force decided to release their harmonized

Table 1.3: VDA and VDA 6.1

About the VDA Group	About VDA 6.1
The German Association of the Automotive Industry—Verband der Automobilindustrie e. V (VDA)—consists partly of automobile manufacturers and their development partners, partly of suppliers, and partly of the manufacturers of trailers, body superstructures, and containers. The fact that automobile manufacturers and suppliers are members of a joint association is by no means common at the international level. In many other countries, such different companies belong to separate associations. The advantages of the German model are there for all to see: The partners sit in the same working groups and working parties. The results are direct discussion and rapid decision making.	VDA 6.1 is the German quality management system for the automotive industry. The fourth edition was issued in December of 1998 and it became mandatory for all German car manufacturers on April 1, 1999. Based on ISO 9001:1994, VDA 6.1 included all of the elements in QS-9000, with four further specific requirements: ■ Element 06.3 (Recognition of Product Risk): Risks of the product fulfilling its own function and its effect on the whole assembly. ■ Element Z1.5 (Employee Satisfaction): Employee perception and their needs and expectations can be met through the company's quality approach. ■ Element 07.3 (Quotation Structure): A customer or market may be offered products for purchase or to be made available to own or to use. ■ Element 12.4 (Quality History): The system helps to describe the quality history of customer-supplied product and offers an overview of the situation during a particular period. The VDA requirement has two components: management, and products and processes. A company must achieve an overall level of compliance exceeding 90 percent, with each element achieving a level of compliance of at least 75 percent, to be registered.

Table 1.4—Statements From OEMs on ISO/TS 16949:1999

DaimlerChrysler

Recognition of VDA 6.1 and QS-9000

- Effective immediately, as part of our global procurement and supply strategy at DaimlerChrysler, registration to either VDA 6.1 or QS-9000, including company-specific requirements, will be accepted as quality registration from our suppliers.
- Registration to ISO/TS 16949, including company specifics, will also be accepted as quality registration from our suppliers. This new technical specification may become the quality management standard of the future.

Ford Motor Co.

- For many suppliers, particularly those with multiple international automotive customers, ISO/TS 16949 may represent substantial efficiencies by allowing one audit to satisfy the quality system requirements of QS-9000, VDA 6.1, AVSQ, and EAQF, when coupled with individual company-specific quality requirements and the common automotive registration scheme. The new technical specification may become the single automotive industry quality management standard of the future.

General Motors Global Suppliers

- GM will accept, as optional to QS-9000, a third-party certification to ISO/TS 16949 that meets the following conditions:
  - ❏ The certification scope must include both ISO/TS 16949 and the accompanying ISO/TS 16949 GM customer-specific requirements.
  - ❏ Note that GM does not require you to upgrade your QS-9000 certificate to ISO/TS 16949. However, we strongly recommend that you use your next QS-9000 surveillance audit to upgrade to the ISO/TS 16949 with the above conditions.

General Motors European Operations

New ISO/TS 16949

- Please note that GM will not recognize certification to VDA 6.1, EAQF, or AVSQ as equivalent to QS-9000 or to ISO/TS 16949. In order to be accepted as a supplier for GM, you must provide either a third-party certification to QS-9000, or optional to ISO/TS 16949, as outlined in the attached letter.

Table 1.5—Comparison of ISO 9001:1994, QS-9000 Third Edition, and ISO/TS 16949:1999

Element	ISO 9001:1994 Shall	QS-9000 Third Edition				ISO/TS 16949:1999 Shall	% Increased Over ISO
		Shall	Should	Total	% Increased Over ISO		
4.1	9	22	8	30	233%	39	333%
4.2	9	37	13	50	456%	62	589%
4.3	5	6	1	7	40%	7	40%
4.4	20	37	2	39	95%	34	70%
4.5	9	10	1	11	22%	12	33%
4.6	11	17	4	21	91%	18	64%
4.7	2	3	0	3	50%	3	50%
4.8	3	3	0	3	0%	3	0%
4.9	7	27	5	32	357%	28	300%
4.10	16	32	4	36	125%	23	44%
4.11	16	14	3	17	6%	20	25%
4.12	2	3	0	3	50%	2	0%
4.13	7	17	1	18	157%	18	157%
4.14	5	12	0	12	140%	14	180%
4.15	9	23	0	23	156%	24	167%
4.16	7	12	0	12	71%	8	14%
4.17	6	6	2	8	33%	12	100%
4.18	3	4	1	5	67%	7	133%
4.19	1	2	0	2	100%	3	200%
4.20	2	3	2	5	150%	4	100%
Total	149			337	126%	341	129%

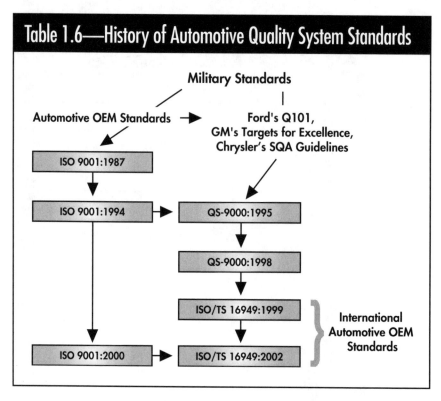

Table 1.6—History of Automotive Quality System Standards

requirements through ISO. In 1999, ISO/TS 16949:1999 was approved by ISO with the two-thirds majority required for ratification as a technical specification. ISO/TS 16949:1999 was based on the 1994 version of ISO 9001 and included requirements from QS-9000, VDA 6.1, EAQF, and AVSQ.

In 1998, the ATF met with the Japanese Automotive Manufacturer's Association (JAMA), which represents all of the Japanese OEMs. The Japanese wanted to join the ATF because they were afraid of being left behind when the U.S. and European automakers joined together in setting quality standards. The task force demurred, being too close to the release of ISO/TS 16949:1999. However, they did agree to invite the Japanese to be a part of the next upgrade of ISO/TS 16949. So, when the second edition of ISO/TS 16949 was developed, the Asian automakers (from Korea, Japan, and Malaysia) became part of the task force, now called the International Automotive Task Force (IATF).

ISO/TS 16949:1999 came out one year after the third edition of QS-9000. Most QS-9000-registered companies had already upgraded their systems and been audited to the new edition of QS-9000 by the time ISO/TS 16949:1999 was released.

ISO/TS 16949:1999 came with some fanfare. (See the U.S. automakers' communication to their supply bases regarding ISO/TS 16949:1999 in table 1.4)

ISO/TS 16949:1999 was similar to QS-9000 in most respects. Table 1.5 compares the two, again counting the "shalls" and "shoulds" between them. In some cases, the number of mandatory requirements actually decreased from QS-9000 to ISO/TS 16949:1999. In some cases, small changes caused an important change to the requirement.

The QS-9000 clauses most changed in ISO/TS 16949:1999 include 4.1, Management responsibility; 4.2, Quality system; 4.14, Corrective and preventive action; 4.17, Internal auditing; and 4.18, Training.

The industry's demand for ISO/TS 16949:1999 was relatively low. The reason for this was twofold: the slow introduction of ISO/TS 16949:1999 to registrars, and the industry's awareness that ISO 9001:2000 was due in December of 1999 (six months after ISO/TS 16949:1999 was introduced). Most quality professionals knew that ISO 9001:2000 would require a paradigm shift in quality concepts. They didn't know that the second edition of ISO/TS 16949 would take three years to be released.

ISO/TS 16949:2002

The second edition of ISO/TS 16949 was destined to be important for two reasons. First, it was going to be an international automotive requirement. Second, it was going to incorporate the latest update to ISO 9001.

ISO/TS 16949:2002 includes ISO 9001:2000 in its entirety. The deadline for ISO 9001:2000 registrations was just 18 months away when ISO/TS 16949:2002 was released. This was a difficult deadline for organizations that wanted to maintain ISO 9001 registration. We will discuss this standard in more detail in chapter 2. (For the history of automotive quality systems standards, see table 1.6.)

Introduction to ISO/TS 16949:2002

SO/TS 16949 includes all of ISO 9001:2000. In ISO/TS 16949, the ISO 9001:2000 requirements appear within closed boxes, clearly delineating the ISO 9001 requirements from ISO/TS 16949's requirements. To understand ISO/TS 16949 fully, the ISO 9001:2000 requirements must also be understood.

INTRODUCTION TO ISO 9001:2000 AND ISO/TS 16949:2002

The ISO 9000 series is updated every five years by ISO Technical Committee 176, which oversees the ISO 9000 series. Although the normal update process triggered the development of ISO 9001:2000, there was a growing understanding that the standard needed to be updated to accommodate a number of user expectations. With that in mind, ISO conducted a worldwide survey of users in 1998. The survey confirmed that the ISO 9000 series needed changes in both structure and content. The survey revealed that the 2000 revision needed to:

- Meet stakeholders' needs
- Be usable by organizations of all sizes
- Be usable by all sectors
- Be simple and easy to understand
- Have enhanced compatibility with ISO 14000
- Connect the quality management system (QMS) to business processes

(Source: Presentation by Jack West, chairman, U.S. TAG to TC 176)

In addition, ISO 9001:2000 advocates the use of other management disciplines to facilitate the achievement of quality objectives. Specifically, the 2000 revision advocates the use of eight quality management principles:

■ Customer focus

■ Leadership

■ Involvement of people

■ Process approach

■ System approach to management

■ Continual improvement

■ Factual approach to decision making

■ Mutually beneficial supplier relationships

A note in ISO/TS 16949 states, "The knowledge and use of the eight management principles referred to in ISO 9000:2000 and ISO 9004:2000 should be demonstrated and cascaded through the organization by top management."

AUTOMOTIVE STAKEHOLDERS

The stakeholders mentioned in ISO/TS 16949 are the international automotive community. The Automotive Task Force (ATF), which wrote QS-9000, expanded its membership to nine voting members and became the International Automotive Task Force (IATF). Consequently, it is now the global automotive community that will provide the direction for future changes to ISO/TS 16949.

The IATF will update ISO/TS 16949 each time ISO 9001 is updated, usually within one year. However, ISO/TS 16949 can be updated independently of ISO 9001 because its review period is shorter than ISO 9001's.

When the IATF decided to update ISO/TS 16949:1999, the primary objectives were to:

■ Harmonize and reduce worldwide automotive standards

■ Integrate ISO/TS 16949:1999 with ISO 9001:2000

■ Improve the application of ISO/TS 16949 worldwide and make audits more consistent

■ Demonstrate to the end user the benefits of implementing ISO/TS 16949

KEY FEATURES OF ISO 9001:2000 AND ISO/TS 16949:2002

ISO 9001:2000 and ISO/TS 16949:2002 are quite different in intent, scope, and structure from their predecessors. They are different in the following respects:

■ *There is more emphasis on processes and a process focus.* This signals that focusing on the individual sections and clauses of ISO/TS 16949 is not recommended. This distinction is obvious when all corporate procedures are titled and arranged according to QS-9000. Some QS-9000-registered organizations didn't benefit from the requirement because they focused on writing procedures that met each of QS-9000's clauses without focusing on improvement.

   A process focus means that the organization has identified the processes used to actually run the business—whether it be sales, accounting, business planning, or delivery. ISO/TS 16949 goes beyond ISO 9001:2000 by classifying and identifying customer-oriented processes, management-oriented processes, and support-oriented processes.

■ *ISO/TS 16949 is customer-focused.* Although customer satisfaction was included in QS-9000, understanding customer's needs and expectations was not fully realized by QS-9000 to the degree that it is understood and linked to objectives by ISO/TS 16949.

■ *Quality objectives are required to be established at relevant functions and levels and to be measurable.* The requirement for objectives is not new to automotive standards. QS-9000 required short- and long-term goals in clause 4.1.4, Business plan. However, the objectives did not need to be measurable or deployed to the relevant function and levels. If objectives are to be measurable, the expectation is that the effectiveness of a QMS be tested by the achievement of measurable objectives.

■ *Quality planning includes consideration of processes, resources, and continual improvement.* Quality planning (clause 5.4.2) is no longer simply about defining and documenting how quality requirements will be met; it's about top management ensuring that the resources needed to achieve quality objectives are identified and planned. Quality planning is now more akin to business planning. This means that an effective QMS should have a business plan.

Again, the requirement for business plans is not new to users of QS-9000 and other automotive standards. However, the need to consider processes (clause 4.1) is new to users of QS-9000. (See clause 5.4.2, Quality planning.)

Management is no longer simply required to review the QMS to ensure continuing suitability and effectiveness during management review (clause 5.6.1); it must now also evaluate the need for changes to the QMS. Outputs from management review are now required to include improvements. In other words, action is now expected.

ISO 9001:2000's management review requirements affect ISO/TS 16949 dramatically. ISO/TS 16949 adds more than twenty business categories to the management review process.

The scope of what used to be inspection and testing has been expanded to include measuring and monitoring of customer satisfaction, internal audits, processes, and products. The analysis of data (clause 8.4) has also been added. Instead of simply checking product (or service) at various stages to verify that the specified requirements for the product are met, an organization now must measure processes and products, and analyze the data resulting from such measurements. The purpose of the analysis is to determine the continuing suitability and effectiveness of the QMS and to identify improvements that can be made. There is a new emphasis on being proactive, the beginning of continual improvement.

Again, this isn't a change from QS-9000, in which analysis of data was required (clause 4.1.5). However, this was only applicable for quality and operational measurables, whereas analysis of data in ISO/TS 16949 (clause 8.4) is broader. Another key addition to ISO/TS 16949 is the customer satisfaction supplemental measurables, in which outgoing quality and delivery (among other metrics) are specifically required to be measured and monitored to ensure customer satisfaction.

All of these differences suggest that a QMS must now have much more of a business focus and must drive measurable improvement toward specific objectives. To the extent that it may have been true in the past, it will no longer be satisfactory simply to have a well-documented QMS.

Senior management must realize that ISO/TS 16949 covers many areas which were previously not found in the domain of senior management. About 33 percent of the auditors' time will be spent auditing top management for the requirements.

PROCESS MODEL

ISO 9001:2000 encourages organizations to adopt a process approach to quality management. Conceptually, the standard describes one approach to a QMS, which is shown in the Quality Management Process Model in figure 2.1.

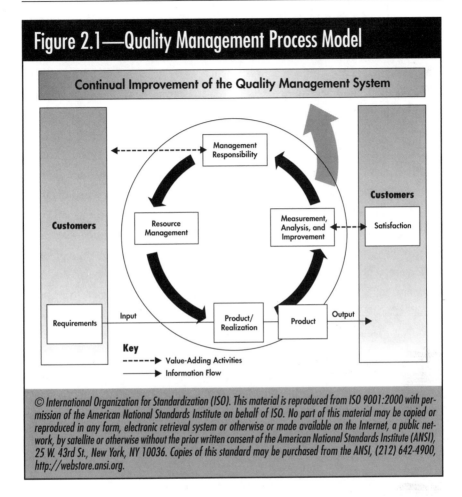

Figure 2.1—Quality Management Process Model

Continual Improvement of the Quality Management System

Management Responsibility

Customers

Resource Management

Measurement, Analysis, and Improvement

Customers

Satisfaction

Requirements

Input

Product/Realization

Product

Output

Key

------▶ Value-Adding Activities

———▶ Information Flow

The process model presents ISO 9001:2000 and ISO/TS 16949 requirements as a linked business process in which input is customer requirements and output is customer satisfaction. When compared with the traditional view of ISO 9001:1994 and QS-9000 as a series of disconnected elements, this is a tremendous step forward. The new process model more accurately represents the way most businesses actually work, whether they document the process or not.

The process model begins with management responsibility (section 5). Management is required to set the course for the business. It does so by studying customer needs and expectations and formulating a quality policy (a mission statement) and specific quality objectives (business objectives) relevant to the customers' requirements. Management is then required to develop a plan of action to achieve the objectives using quality planning (or business planning) and define the QMS (or business system) that will carry out these plans. To do this, the business processes must be defined. This definition needs to include processes to meet the requirements of the standard, customer requirements, and customer product requirements. Finally, management is required to review the plan's progress toward objectives on a regular basis.

The next step of the process model is resource management (section 6.0). During this step, the organization must identify and provide all of the resources required for achieving the quality plan. These resources may include trained and qualified personnel, facilities, equipment, and a working environment that meets customer requirements.

In the next step, product realization (section 7.0), the organization must describe the requirements of running the business to produce products and services that meet customer requirements. This step requires that processes which add value to the product or service (i.e., realization processes) are properly planned to achieve quality objectives. This includes all processes, from design to delivery. The realization processes must be defined, documented, verified, and validated. Customer requirements must be identified and reviewed, and products and services designed to meet those requirements. Then the products and services must be produced and/or delivered in a controlled fashion and according to the plan.

The last step in this four-step process model is measurement, analysis, and improvement (section 8.0). Four types of measurement should be taken:

- Customer satisfaction
- Internal audit
- Processes
- Products

The data from these measurements should be used in three ways:

- To ensure that customer requirements are met
- To solve problems
- To improve the QMS

This last step involves analyzing and using data to identify and track improvement actions. The information generated by this process must be reviewed by management on a regular basis.

Table 2.1—Comparison Between QS-9000, ISO/TS 16949:1999 and ISO/TS 16949:2002

QS-9000 Third Edition	ISO/TS 16949:1999	ISO/TS 16949:2002
4.1 – Management Responsibility		
Not present	4.1.1.2 Objectives	5.4.1.1 Quality objectives— Supplemental
4.1.6 Customer satisfaction	4.1.1.3 Customer satisfaction	8.2.1.1 Customer satisfaction— Supplemental
Not present	4.1.1.4 Continuous improvement	Removed
4.2.5 Continuous improvement	4.1.1.4 Remaining requirements	8.5.1.1 Continual improvement of the organization
4.1.2 f Responsibility and authority	4.1.2.1.2 Customer representative	5.5.2.1 Customer representative
4.1.2 a as Note	4.1.2.1.3 Quality responsibility	5.5.1.1 Responsibility of quality
Not present	4.1.2.2.2 Shift resources	5.5.1.1 Responsibility of quality
4.1.2.4 Organizational interfaces	4.1.2.4 Organizational interfaces	7.3.1.1 Multidisciplinary approach 7.2.3.1 Customer communication— Supplemental
4.1.3.1 Management review Not present	4.1.3.2 Management review— Supplemental 4.2.8 Quality system performance (Above elements are moved to 5.6.1.1)	5.6.1.1 Quality management system performance 5.6.2.1 Review input—Supplemental
4.1.4 Business plan	4.1.4 Business plan	Removed
4.1.5 Analysis and use of company level data	4.1.5 Analysis and use of company level data	8.4.1 Analysis and use of data
Not present	4.1.6 Employee motivation, empowerment and satisfaction	6.2.2.4 Employee motivation and empowerment
4.2.3.4 Product safety	4.1.7.1 Product safety	6.4.1 Personnel safety to achieve product quality
Not present	4.1.7.2 Regulations	7.2.1 Determination of requirements relating to product
4.2 Quality Systems		
4.2.1 & 4.2.2 General and quality system procedures	4.2.2.2 Quality system documentation	Removed

QS-9000 Third Edition	ISO/TS 16949:1999	ISO/TS 16949:2002
4.2.3 Quality planning	4.2.3.2 Quality plan requirements	7.1.1 Planning of product realization—Supplemental
4.2.3.1 Advanced product quality planning	4.2.4.1 Product realization—General	7.1 Product realization 7.1.3 Confidentiality
Not present	4.2.4.2 Measurements	7.3.4.1 Monitoring
Not present	4.2.4.3 Review cycle	Removed
4.2.3.1 Advanced product quality planning & 4.1.2.4 Organizational interfaces	4.2.4.4 Multidisciplinary approach	7.3.1.1 Multidisciplinary approach
Not there	4.2.4.5 Tools and techniques—Initial process studies	8.2.3.1 Monitoring and measurement manufacturing processes
4.2.3.5 PFMEA 4.2.3.7 Control plan 4.2.3.6 Mistake proofing	4.2.4.5 Tools and techniques—FMEAs/CPs and mistake proofing	7.3.3.1 Product design outputs—Supplemental 7.3.3.2 Manufacturing process design outputs 7.3.2.2 Manufacturing process design input
4.4.2.1 Required skills	4.2.4.6 Computer-aided design—Skills	6.2.2.1 Product design skills
4.2.3.2 Special characteristics	4.2.4.7 Special characteristics	7.3.2.3 Special characteristics
4.2.3.3 Feasibility reviews	4.2.4.8 Feasibility reviews	7.2.2.2 Organization manufacturing feasibility
Not there	4.2.4.9.1 Management of process design—General	Removed
Not there	4.2.4.9.2 Process design inputs	7.3.2.2 Manufacturing process design input
Not there	4.2.4.9.3 Process design output	7.3.3.2 Manufacturing process design output
Not there	4.2.4.9.4 Process verification	7.3.5 Design and development verification
4.2.3.7 Control plan	4.2.4.10 Control plan	7.5.1.1 Control plan
4.2.4 Product approval process	4.2.4.11 Product approval process	7.3.6.3 Product approval process

QS-9000 Third Edition	ISO/TS 16949:1999	ISO/TS 16949:2002
4.2.4 Product approval process	4.2.4.11 Product approval process	7.1.4 Change control
4.2.6.1 Facilities, equipment and process planning effectiveness	4.2.5 Plant, facility and equipment planning	6.3.1 Plant, facility and equipment planning
4.2.6.2 Tooling management	4.2.6 Tooling management	7.5.1.5 Management of production tooling
4.2.5 Continuous improvement	4.2.7 Process improvement	8.5.1.2 Manufacturing process improvement
Not there	4.2.8 Quality system performance	5.6.1.1 Quality management system performance 5.1.1 Process efficiency
4.3 Contract review		
Not present	4.3.2.2 Review—Supplemental	Removed
4.4 Design control		
Not there	4.4 Design control—Important (treating process design under 4.4)	7.3 Design and development
4.4.2.1 Required skills	4.4.2.2 Required skills	6.2.2.1 Product design skills
Not there	4.4.2.3 Research and development	Removed
Not there	4.4.4.2 Reliability objectives	7.3.2.1 Product design inputs
4.4.1.1 Use of design data	4.4.4.3 Use of information	7.3.2.1 Product design inputs
Not there	4.4.5.2 Design optimization	7.3.3.1 Product design outputs— Supplemental
4.4.8.1 Design validation— Supplemental	4.4.8.2 Design validation—Supplemental 4.4.8.3 Prototype program	7.3.6.1 Design and development validation—Supplemental
4.4.10 Customer prototype support	4.4.9.2 Evaluation of design change	7.3.6.2 Prototype program
4.4.9.1 Design changes—Supplemental 4.4.9.2 Design change impact		7.1.4 Change control
4.5 Document and data control		
4.5.2 Note	4.5.2.1 Note	Removed
4.5.2.1 Engineering specification	4.5.2.2 Engineering specifications	4.2.3.1 Engineering specifications

QS-9000 Third Edition	ISO/TS 16949:1999	ISO/TS 16949:2002
4.6 Purchasing		
4.6.1 Note	4.6.1.1 Note	Note removed and added two notes under 7.4.1 Purchasing process
4.6.1.1 Approved materials for ongoing production	4.6.1.2 Customer approved subcontractors	7.4.1.3 Customer approved sources
4.6.1.2 Regulatory compliance	4.6.1.3 Regulatory compliance	7.4.1.1 Regulatory compliance
4.6.2.1 Subcontractor development	4.6.2.2 Subcontractor development	7.4.1.2 Supplier quality management system development
4.6.2.2 Scheduling subcontractors	4.6.2.3 Scheduling subcontractors	7.4.3.2 Supplier monitoring
4.7 Control of customer supplied product		
4.7.1 Customer owned tooling	4.7.2 Customer owned tooling	7.5.4.1 Customer owned production tooling
4.8 Product identification and traceability		
4.8 Note	4.8	7.5.3 Product identification and traceability 7.5.3.1 Identification and traceability—Supplemental
4.9 Process control		
4.9.b.1 Cleanliness of premises	4.9.1.2 Cleanliness of premises	6.4.2 Cleanliness of premises
4.9.b.2 Contingency plans	4.9.1.3 Contingency plans	6.3.2 Contingency plans
4.9.d.1 Designation of special characteristics	4.9.1.4 Designation of special characteristics	7.2.1.1 Customer designated special characteristics
4.9.g.1 Preventive maintenance	4.9.1.5 Preventive maintenance	7.5.1.4 Preventive and predictive maintenance
4.9.1 Process monitoring and operator instructions	4.9.2 Job instructions	7.5.1.2 Work instructions
4.9.2 Maintaining process control 4.9.5 Process changes	4.9.3 Maintaining process control	8.2.3.1 Monitoring and measurement of processes—Supplemental
4.9.4 Verification of job setups	4.9.4 Verification of job setups	7.5.1.3 Verification of job setups
4.9.6 Appearance items	4.9.5 Appearance items	8.2.4.2 Appearance items
4.9.3 Modified process control requirements	Removed	Removed

QS-9000 Edition	ISO/TS 16949:1999	ISO/TS 16949:2002
4.10 Inspection and testing		
Not present	4.10.1.1 Note	8.2.4 Monitoring and measurement of product
4.10.1.1 Acceptance criteria	4.10.1.2 Acceptance criteria	7.1.2 Acceptance criteria
4.10.2.4 Incoming product quality	4.10.2.4 Incoming product quality	7.4.3.1 Incoming product quality
4.10.4.1 Layout inspection and functional testing	4.10.4.2 Layout inspection and functional testing	8.2.4.1 Layout and functional testing
4.10.6 Supplier laboratory requirements 4.10.7 Accredited laboratories	4.10.6 Laboratory requirements	7.6.3 Laboratory requirements 7.6.3.1 Internal labs 7.6.3.2 External labs
4.11 Control of inspection, measuring and test equipment		
4.11.4 Measurement system analysis	4.11.1.2 Measurement system analysis	7.6.1 Measurement system analysis
4.11.3 Inspection, measuring and test equipments records	4.11.3 Records	7.6.2 Calibration records
4.12 Inspection and test status		
4.12 Note 4.12.1 Supplemental verification	4.12 Inspection and test status	7.5.3 Product identification and traceability
4.13 Control of nonconforming product		
4.13.1.1 Suspect material or product 4.13.1.2 Visual identification	4.13.1.2 Suspect material or product	8.3.1 Control of nonconforming product—Supplemental
4.13.2.1 Prioritized reduction plans	4.13.1.3 Corrective action plan	8.3.3 Customer information
4.13.3 Control of reworked product	4.13.3 Control of reworked product	8.3.2 Control of reworked product
4.13.4 Engineering approved product authorization	4.13.4 Engineering approved authorization	8.3.4 Customer waiver
4.14 Corrective and preventive action		
4.14.1.1 Problem solving methods	4.14.1.2 Problem solving	8.5.2.1 Problem solving
4.14.1.2 Mistake proofing	4.14.1.3 Mistake proofing	8.5.2.2 Error proofing
4.14.2.2 Corrective action impact	4.14.2.2 Corrective action impact	8.5.2.3 Corrective action impact
4.14.2.1 Returned product test/analysis	4.14.2.3 Returned product test/analysis	8.5.2.4 Rejected product test/analysis

QS-9000 Third Edition	ISO/TS 16949:1999	ISO/TS 16949:2002
4.15 Handling, storage, packaging, preservation and delivery		
4.15.3.1 Inventory	4.15.3.2 Inventory	7.5.5.1 Storage and inventory
4.15.4.1 Customer packaging standards	4.15.4.2 Customer packaging standards	7.1.1 Planning of product realization— Supplemental
4.15.4.2 Labeling	4.15.4.3 Labeling	7.1.1
4.15.6.1 Supplier delivery performance monitoring	4.15.6.2 Performance monitoring of supplier delivery	8.2.1.1 Customer satisfaction— Supplemental
4.15.6.2 Production scheduling	4.15.6.3 Production scheduling	7.5.1.6 Production scheduling
4.15.6.3 Electronic communication	4.15.6.4 Electronic communication	7.1.1 Customer satisfaction— Supplemental
4.15.6.4 Shipment notification system	4.15.6.5 Shipment notification system	7.1.1 Customer satisfaction— Supplemental
4.16 Control of quality records		
4.16.1 Record retention	4.16.2 Record retention	4.2.4.1 Record retention
4.17 Internal quality audits		
4.17.1 Internal audit schedules	4.17.2.1 Internal quality audits— Supplemental—General	8.2.2.4 – Internal audit plans
Not there	4.17.2.2 System audit	8.2.2.1 Quality management system audit
Not there	4.17.2.3 Process audit	8.2.2.2 Manufacturing process audit
4.10.4.2 Final product audit	4.17.2.4 Product audit	8.2.2.3 Product audit
Not there	4.17.3 Auditor qualification	8.2.2.5 Internal auditor qualification
4.18 Training		
4.18. Training	4.18.1 Training	6.2.2.2 Training
4.18.1 Training effectiveness	4.18.2 Training effectiveness	6.2.2.c
		6.2.2.2 Training
Not there	4.18.3 Training on the job	6.2.2.3 Training on the job
4.19 Servicing		
4.19 Servicing—Note	4.19.1 Servicing—Note	Note removed
4.19.1 Feedback of information from service	4.19.2 Feedback of information from service	7.5.1.7 Feedback of information from service
Not there	4.19.3 Servicing agreement with customer	7.5.1.8 Servicing agreement with customer

QS-9000 Third Edition	ISO/TS 16949:1999	ISO/TS 16949:2002
4.20 Statistical techniques		
4.20.3 Selection of statistical tools	4.20.3 Identification of statistical tools	8.1.1 Identification of statistical tools
4.20.4 Knowledge of basic statistical concepts	4.20.4 Knowledge of basic statistical concepts	8.1.2 Knowledge of basic statistical concepts

The process model anticipates that the four steps will be repeated continuously to drive overall improvement of the business. This rhythm closely matches that which most businesses already naturally follow. The difference in the new process model is that it adds structure and discipline to the process.

ISO/TS 16949 has many additions to ISO 9001:2000's requirements. For the most part, the additions to sections 4.0, Quality management system; 5.0, Management responsibility; and 6.0, Resource management, are less significant than the additions to section 7.0, Product realization, and section 8.0, Measurement, analysis, and improvement.

Some of the changes in ISO/TS 16949 are not in the technical specification itself—namely the automotive process approach, which the IATF says is a direct application of the process model. This approach defines categories of processes, starting with customer-oriented processes (COPs), that have an input from the customer and an output back to the customer. It also defines a line of sight between the customer to the organization. This definition is useful, especially when describing processes within large corporations. This approach further defines COPs, management-oriented processes (MOPs), and support-oriented processes (SOPs), which will be covered in more detail in chapter 3.

KEY DEFINITIONS

Several key terms have either been added or redefined in ISO 9000:2000. These redefined and added terms include "quality," "characteristic," "product," "requirement," and "interested party." This is significant because the new definitions represent both an expansion in the scope of ISO 9000:2000 and a change in its intent.

ISO 9000:2000 redefined *quality* as the "degree to which a set of inherent characteristics (3.5.1) fulfills requirements (3.1.2)." Note that the term "quality" can be used with adjectives such as poor, good, or excellent. Also note that the term "inherent," as opposed to "assigned," is defined as existing in something, especially as a permanent characteristic.

Quality cannot be fully understood without first understanding the definitions of the terms "characteristic," "product," "requirements," and "interested party."

A *characteristic* is a distinguishing feature. There are various classes of characteristics:

■ Physical (e.g., mechanical, electrical, chemical, or biological)

■ Sensory (e.g., smell, touch, taste, sight, or hearing)

■ Behavioral (e.g., courtesy, honesty, or veracity)

■ Temporal (e.g., punctuality, reliability, or availability)

■ Ergonomic (e.g., a linguistic or physiological characteristic, or related to human safety)

■ Functional (e.g., range of a plane)

Quality is about cost, technology, delivery, and all other aspects important to the customer. In other words, quality is about meeting the needs and expectations of the customer. This means all of the customer's needs and expectations, not just product quality.

A *product* is the result of a process. There are four generic product categories:

■ Hardware (e.g., engine mechanical part)

■ Software (e.g., computer program)

■ Services (e.g., transport)

■ Processed materials (e.g., lubricant)

A *requirement* is a need or expectation that is stated, customarily implied, or obligatory. A qualifier may be used to denote a specific type of requirement (e.g., product requirement, quality system requirement, or customer requirement.) A specified requirement is one that is stated, such as in a document (clause 2.7.1). Requirements may be generated by different interested parties (clause 2.3.7).

An *interested party* is a person or group with an interest in the performance or success of an organization (clause 2.3.1). Customers (clause 2.3.5), owners, employees, suppliers (clause 2.3.6), bankers, unions, partners, or society are all interested parties. A group may consist of an organization, a part thereof, or more than one organization.

A *customer* is an organization (clause 3.3.1) or person who receives a product (clause 3.4.2). Examples include consumers, clients, end-users, retailers, beneficiaries, and purchasers. Note that a customer can be internal or external to the organization.

A *site* is a location at which value-added manufacturing processes occur.

A *remote location* is a location that supports sites and at which nonproduction processes occur.

ACHIEVING QUALITY

The ultimate goal of a QMS is customer satisfaction. The system must deliver quality. As noted previously, quality is ultimately the ability of a set of inherent characteristics of a product, system, or process to fulfill the needs and expectations of customers.

To achieve quality, the needs and expectations of customers must be determined. These needs and expectations, or requirements, must be translated into classes of characteristics (e.g., physical, sensory, behavioral, temporal, ergonomic, or functional).

ISO 9001:1994 recognized the customer as the purchaser and described customer requirements as physical and functional. ISO/TS 16949 has broadened the scope of what "requirements" means and who customers are. The starting point for an organization implementing ISO/TS 16949 is to identify its customers and then determine their requirements.

ISO 9001:2000 and ISO/TS 16949 are profound in their importance because they change the way quality is handled within the modern organization. They require organizations to map characteristics derived from customer expectations of products, systems, or processes. They describe four types of products: hardware, software, services, and processed materials. According to ISO 9001:2000 and ISO/TS 16949, customer and interested party requirements can only be derived from inherent characteristics in products, systems, and processes.

Be careful when comparing ISO 9001:1994 or QS-9000 to ISO 9001:2000 or ISO/TS 16949:2002. The new definitions of terms like "quality" or "characteristic" are not interchangeable with the old definitions. Substituting the word "business" wherever the word "quality" appears in ISO 9001:2000 and ISO/TS 16949 will help you understand the magnitude of the change in meaning. This book frequently refers to "quality" as "business/quality," including substituting "business management system" (BMS) for "quality management system" (QMS).

QUALITY MANAGEMENT SYSTEMS APPROACH

ISO 9001:2000 and ISO/TS 16949 are designed around what ISO calls the "Quality Management Systems Approach," which is essentially a roadmap of the tasks that need to be completed to implement a successful BMS. The steps of the approach are:

1. Determine the needs and expectations of the customer.
2. Establish a quality policy and quality objectives.
3. Determine the processes and responsibilities necessary to obtain the objectives.
4. Establish measures for the effectiveness of each process toward attaining the objectives.
5. Apply the measures to determine the current effectiveness of each process.
6. Determine means of preventing nonconformities and eliminating their causes.
7. Look for opportunities to improve the effectiveness and efficiencies of the processes.
8. Determine and prioritize improvements that can provide optimum results.
9. Plan for the strategies, processes, and resources to deliver the identified improvements.
10. Implement the plan.
11. Monitor the effects of the improvements.
12. Assess the results against the expected outcomes.
13. Review the improvement activities to determine appropriate follow-up actions.

CONTINUAL IMPROVEMENT

Continual improvement is a key addition to ISO 9001:2000, which defines improvement as, "the actions taken to enhance the features and characteristics of products and/or services, and to increase the effectiveness of processes used to produce and deliver them." Continual means that there should be a never-ending process of improvement. In the context of ISO/TS 16949, it means that the organization should continually move through the process model steps.

The continual improvement steps as defined by ISO 9001:2000 are:

1. Define, measure, and analyze the existing situation.
2. Establish the objectives for improvement.
3. Search for possible solutions.
4. Evaluate these solutions.
5. Implement these solutions.

6. Measure, verify, and analyze results of the implementation.

7. Formalize the changes.

Furthermore, ISO/TS 16949 and ISO 9001:2000 require organizations to use the quality policy, quality objectives, management review, analysis of data, and other methods for continual improvement. The need for continual improvement to be data-driven is new to automotive standards.

DIFFERENCES BETWEEN ISO/TS 16949:2002 AND QS-9000

The most significant difference between ISO/TS 16949 and QS-9000 is the customer and process focus required by ISO/TS 16949. Seven major changes and many minor changes have been identified between ISO/TS 16949 and QS-9000. The major changes are customer focus, process focus, process documentation, deployed objectives, expanded and integrated management review, inclusion of process design and development, and customer-specific requirements. The minor changes are numerous and significant. This book covers ten of them in detail. They include internal communication, resource allocation, human resources, product realization documentation, purchasing, and others. (See chapter 3.)

To understand, implement, or audit ISO/TS 16949, you need an understanding of five documents: ISO/TS 16949:2002, the Certification Scheme for ISO/TS 16949:2002, the QSA Checklist to ISO/TS 16949:2002, the IATF Guidance to ISO/TS 16949, and the customer-specific requirements. Although the five reference manuals in QS-9000 are not mandated by ISO/TS 16949, their use is *required* by DaimlerChrysler, Ford, and GM. The five reference manuals are:

■ *Advanced Product Quality Planning* (APQP)

■ *Failure Mode and Effects Analysis* (FMEA)

■ *Measurement Systems Analysis* (MSA)

■ *Production Part Approval Process* (PPAP)

■ *Statistical Process Control* (SPC)

Some key differences (in addition to the process focus and customer focus) include the classification of processes (i.e., COPs, MOPs, and SOPs), the process auditing approach, and the performance requirements. The COPs, MOPs, and SOPs were introduced earlier in this chapter and will be covered in detail in chapter 4.

Process auditing will be covered briefly in chapter 7. The IATF considers process auditing to be the key difference in auditing between QS-9000 and ISO/TS 16949.

Case Study of an International Tier-One Supplier

QSTS had a contract with an accredited registrar qualified to conduct QS-9000 registration assessments, but the registrar was not on the International Automotive Oversight Bureau's (IAOB) list of registrars qualified to conduct ISO/TS 16949 assessments. At the end of the registrar's contract for QS-9000, QSTS decided to switch to a registrar included on the IAOB list because it planned on transitioning to ISO/TS 16949:2002. QSTS was confident it could easily transition to both ISO 9001:2000 and ISO/TS 16949:2002, because it had already been working for more than five years on meeting excellence standards such as the Malcolm Baldrige National Quality Award.

The new registrar's initial audit provided for a QMS assessment that would permit a registration transition from ISO 9001:1994 (and the third edition of QS-9000) to ISO 9001:2000 and ISO/TS 16949:1999. However, the audit was a wake-up call instead. The assessment of QSTS ended up identifying several major nonconformances, including one that required the organization to align itself with a site (it was technically a "remote location") despite the fact that QSTS had a design center, sales, purchasing and some senior management located in the United States.

Some of the nonconformances resulted from a lack of preparation by the previous registrar's auditors. In fact, they had not completed a document review (desktop audit) prior to the on-site audit. The other nonconformances existed because the organization was not prepared for conformance to both ISO 9001:2000 and ISO/TS 16949:1999. QSTS has a few special circumstances that need to be mentioned (even though they do not excuse legitimate nonconformances), including that it had ten to fifteen product lines located in the United States, although several of the business units they report to are located in Europe. What then is the definition of "top management"?

After the poor showing on the audit, QSTS contacted a consultant, Omnex Inc. QSTS and Omnex collectively decided that it didn't make sense for QSTS pursue ISO 9001:2000 and ISO/TS 16949:1999, but that it should instead pursue ISO 9001:2000 and ISO/TS 16949:2002, which had just become available in final draft form.

INTERNAL PRESSURE ON THE IATF

There is intense internal pressure within DaimlerChrysler, Ford, and GM regarding QS-9000 and ISO/TS 16949. This pressure occurs on several fronts. First, the question is often raised whether second-party or third-party auditing is better. Second, when quality problems occur at the supplier level, there is an immediate indictment of the registration process and the added value of ISO/TS 16949. Third, there is a pressure from groups that manage the supply base to allow suppliers to dictate their own requirements rather than follow ISO/TS 16949.

This internal pressure to increase the audit quality and improve added value has led the IATF to reduce the number of registrars who can audit ISO/TS 16949 from more than 140 for QS-9000 to a few more than 50 for ISO/TS 16949. Furthermore, the auditors who can audit ISO/TS 16949 are required to have considerable experience auditing to either QS-9000 or ISO/TS 16949. These changes will undoubtedly result in much better auditing of ISO/TS 16949.

Some QS-9000-registered companies are in for a shock when they begin the ISO/TS 16949 transition process. Due to the uneven quality of third-party registrars, depending upon their registrar, they may not have received a true QS-9000 audit. One large tier-one electronic supplier had five major nonconformances when it switched from a QS-9000-accredited registrar to an ISO/TS 16949-accredited registrar. These major nonconformances to QS-9000 had gone undetected by the previous registrar.

The second major change resulting from internal pressure are the performance requirements (clause 8.2.1.1) for the automotive supply chain in ISO/TS 16949. Both the organization implementing ISO/TS 16949 and its suppliers need to adhere to four performance measurements:

- Delivered part quality performance
- Customer disruptions (including field returns)
- Delivery schedule performance (including premium freight)
- Customer notification related to quality or delivery issues

These internal pressures on the IATF, and hence on the International Automotive Oversight Bureau (IAOB) and registrars, will undoubtedly improve the overall results of the auditing process.

Chapter 3

Becoming Process-Focused

The most significant changes that organizations will face when transitioning from QS-9000 or ISO/TS 16949:1999 to ISO/TS 16949:2002 are contained in seventeen clauses and subclauses found in ISO 9001:2000 and ISO/TS 16949:2002.

Table 3.1 shows the key challenges when transitioning from QS-9000 to ISO/TS 16949. The first two are the process focus and the customer focus required by ISO/TS 16949. Seven major changes and ten minor changes are identified and explained in the next few chapters. Table 3.1 shows the chapter numbers and titles covering the transition challenges. Chapter 9 will discuss the documentation requirements for ISO/TS 16949, and chapter 10 will discuss how an organization should transition to ISO/TS 16949.

4.1 QUALITY MANAGEMENT SYSTEM— GENERAL REQUIREMENTS

Clause 4.1 requires an organization to go beyond QS-9000 and identify the processes within its hierarchical organizational structure. The organizational structure and the chain of command follow Frederick Winslow Taylor's theory of specialization—known in the automotive industry as organizational silos or chimneys (shown in figure 3.1.)

In ISO/TS 16949, products are realized by processes. This requires the organization to identify its product realization and support processes. These processes aren't just for the product; they are also responsible for satisfying the customer.

In determining the processes, one of the first tasks facing the organization is the identification of the implementation's scope. In other words, which parts of the organ-

Table 3.1—The Seventeen Key ISO/TS 16949:2002 Transition Challenges for QS-9000-Registered Organizations

Clause/Subclause	Influenced by	Challenges	Chapter Reference
4.1 Quality management system—General requirements	ISO 9001:2000	Requirements for process map (or equivalent), process management, customer-oriented processes, support processes, and process characteristics	3
4.2 Documentation requirements	ISO 9001:2000 and New	Document processes and their interface. Document COPs, MOPs, and SOPs	Scope 3 & 9
5.2 Management responsibility—Customer focus	ISO 9001:2000	Decision on customer vs. interested parties. Need for process to gather "needs and expectations" of customers/interested parties	4
5.4.1 Planning—Quality objectives	ISO 9001:2000 and ISO/TS 16949:1999	Deployed objectives addressing customer expectations	4
5.5 Internal communication	ISO 9001:2000	Creation of internal communication processes suitable to organization	6
5.6 Management review	ISO 9001:2000 and ISO/TS 16949:1999	Revision of previous management review process. ISO/TS 16949:2002 adds additional items to be reviewed.	4
6.1 Resource management—Provision of resources	ISO 9001:2000	Establishment of resource allocation process	6

Table 3.1—The Seventeen Key ISO/TS 16949:2002 Transition Challenges for QS-9000-Registered Organizations

Clause/Subclause	Influenced by	Challenges	Chapter Reference
6.2 Human resources (particularly 6.2.2.3 and 6.2.2.4)	ISO 9001:2000 and ISO/TS 16949:1999	Provision of job competency, on-the-job training, and employee motivation and empowerment	6
7. Product realization	ISO 9001:2000	Documents for "effective control" of all processes in process map	9
7.1.4 Change control	New	Minor change for most suppliers	7
7.2 Customer-specific requirements	QS-9000	Additional requirements for suppliers are included in the customer-specific requirements, especially Ford.	8
7.3 Design and development	New	Inclusion of design and development of processes, not just product (note required development and use of FMEAs)	5
7.4 Purchasing	New	Inclusion of service suppliers in coverage and use of suppliers monitored indicators. ISO 9001:2000 registration of suppliers	5

Table 3.1—The Seventeen Key ISO/TS 16949:2002 Transition Challenges for QS-9000-Registered Organizations

Clause/Subclause	Influenced by	Challenges	Chapter Reference
8.2.1 Monitoring and measure-ment—Customer satisfaction	ISO 9001:2000	Customer rating for quality and delivery insufficient: monitoring of "customer perceptions" of quality. Importance of customer satisfaction—supplemental requirements, including delivered part quality and schedule performance to IATF	4
8.2.2 Internal Audit	ISO/TS 16949:1999	Manufacturing process and product audits based on COPs and process approach	7
8.2.3 Monitoring and measurement of processes	ISO 9001:2000 and ISO/TS 16949:1999	Process studies on manufactur-ing processes. Measurement of all processes is process map	7
8.4 Analysis of data	ISO 9001:2000	Increased scope from QS-9000	7

ization fall under the jurisdiction of ISO/TS 16949? Which of the organization's departments should be included, and which ones should be excluded? Can research-and-development and sales offices be left out?

Figure 3.1—Chimney Diagram

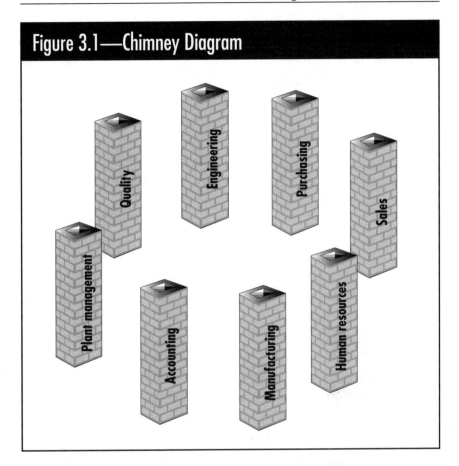

DETERMINING THE SCOPE

Two QS-9000 paradigms need to be discarded at this stage. One is that the organization can exclude processes not specified in ISO/TS 16949. Clause 1.2, Application, specifies that only processes which don't "affect the organization's ability, or responsibility, to provide product that meets customer and applicable regulatory requirements" can be excluded from the quality management system's (QMS) scope.

It's questionable for organizations to leave out research-and-development centers or sales offices because customer needs cannot be met without them. Furthermore, ISO/TS 16949 has expanded the applicability of clause 7.3, Design and development, to both product and process design by including clauses 7.3.2.2, Manufacturing process design input, and 7.3.3.2, Manufacturing process design output. No organization implementing ISO/TS 16949 can exclude clause 7.3 because every product and service parts supplier has production processes that need to be designed and developed using the QMS.

The other defunct paradigm from QS-9000 is that an organization doesn't have to control outsourced processes. The last paragraph of clause 4.1, General requirements clearly states that when the organization "chooses to outsource any process that affects product conformity with requirements, the organization shall ensure control over such processes." QS-9000's clause 4.6.2, Evaluation of subcontractors, requires an organization to exercise control over its suppliers, but only to meet customer requirements for subcontractors and only to the extent necessary to ensure supplier-provided product meets specifications relative to the organization's product.

With ISO/TS 16949, an organization must include outsourced processes within its process map and QMS whenever a supplier can affect the organization's product, including design, heat treating or plating, or any component of an assembly manufactured by that supplier.

The scope statement is an important requirement for the quality manual (clause 4.2.2). The scope statement carefully describes the standard the organization intends to achieve and details any exclusions claimed. The scope also details sites and remote locations. ISO/TS 16949 allows the organization to omit clause 7.3, Design and development, but only if the organization doesn't actually do product design and development. All other requirements should be met, even if the organization does not currently practice them. In other words, even if the organization doesn't have customer-owned tooling and packaging, it is required to have a process for it.

"Site" and "remote location" refer to the linkage between the manufacturing location and other parts of the organization that support it. Site is defined as the "location at which value-added manufacturing processes occur" (i.e., a manufacturing location). Remote location refers to a "location that supports sites and at which nonproduction processes occur." Examples of remote locations include sales offices, design centers, corporate purchasing, or distribution sites. The key is for the organization to carefully document the processes between the sites and remote locations. The auditor needs to assess the interface between sites and remote locations. (See figure 3.2.)

Is there a clear line of sight between processes entering a corporate location (a remote location) and branching off to other areas to address top management or customer questions/issues?

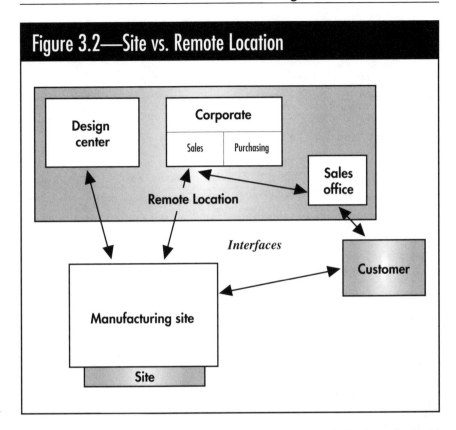

Figure 3.2—Site vs. Remote Location

For a large corporate location, the scope of all entities included in the audit should be covered in the corporate business/quality manual. Local organizations and business units also need to identify the scope (i.e., site vs. remote locations) for their audits. According to the International Automotive Oversight Bureau (IAOB), there is a ninety-day time limit between the site audit and the remote location(s) audits. This is particularly daunting for organizations with many international locations.

The third determinant of the scope for ISO/TS 16949 is the requirement for the product to be "automotive" in nature. In other words, the product needs to end up in a vehicle, whether it's plastic used in dashboards or steel used in the engine. This is a particular challenge to certain industries that supply several large markets. They would prefer all of their plants to adhere to one business/quality system and one standard.

Once the scope is established, the organization needs to document the high-level processes within the scope.

BECOMING PROCESS-FOCUSED

Becoming process-focused involves implementing four tools or methodologies:

- Process map
- Process list
- Alignment charts
- Business control plans

A process map is a representation of the high-level processes that define an organization. When creating a process map, an organization will need to go beyond ISO/TS 16949's clauses and explain how it truly functions as an organization. How does it design new products? How does it innovate? How does it get customer contracts?

A telltale sign to auditors that a QMS isn't effective is a process map that only includes ISO/TS 16949 clauses. The inherent difference between a process focus and a departmental focus is that a process may move through several departments within an organization. The antithesis to the process approach of ISO 9001:2000 and ISO/TS 16949 is the compliance-driven approach, which implements quality system procedures based solely upon requirements, without any thought of creating systems that actually support and enhance the functioning processes within an organization.

Your organization should evaluate four types of processes for inclusion in the process map:

- Customer-oriented processes (COPs)
- Management-oriented processes (MOPs)
- Support-oriented processes (SOPs)
- ISO/TS 16949 processes

COPs receive input from the customer with output going back to the customer. The product realization process has four COPs: product and process verification/validation, production, delivery, and post-delivery service processes. MOPs are management-related, such as business planning, objectives deployment, and continual improvement. SOPs aid the overall organization and include operations such as training, purchasing, and document control.

ISO/TS 16949 processes obviously relate to ISO/TS 16949 requirements. This category of processes addresses any area of ISO/TS 16949 not covered by the

Figure 3.3—Relationship Among Types of Processes

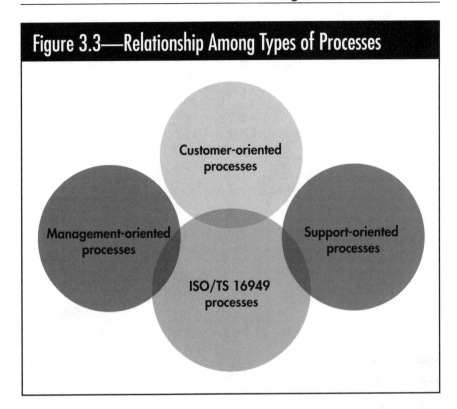

COPs, MOPs, and SOPs. Actually, most ISO/TS 16949 processes are covered by COPs, MOPs, or SOPs. In other words, there is significant overlap among the four types of processes, as shown in figure 3.3.

By definition, a process will be classified as either a COP, MOP, or SOP. After studying the different processes, your organization can create a process map. The process map also can show the sequence and interaction of the various processes. Figure 3.4 illustrates a sample process map.

CREATING A PROCESS MAP

The process map is made up of process blocks, which consist of groups of individual processes. For example, the product realization block would contain the research-and-development, sales, product design, process design, manufacturing, and other related processes. Subsequently, support process blocks or management process blocks would be added to the map. An important process in the management process block is how business strategy, objectives, and management review processes are conducted by the organization.

Figure 3.4—Sample Process Map

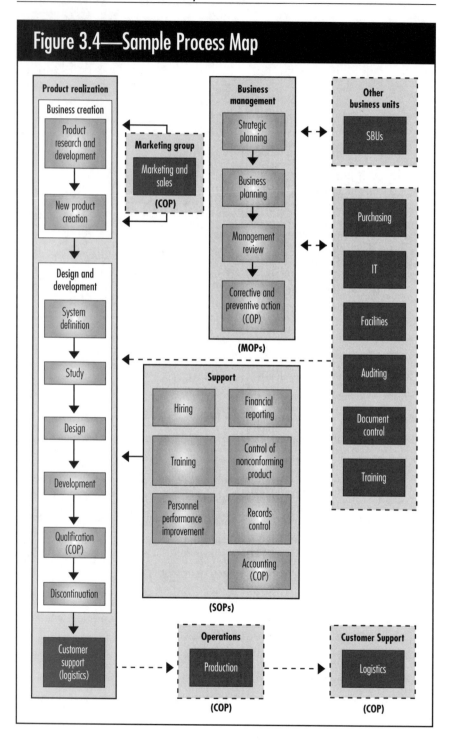

The processes in the process map should be limited to high-level processes that, in turn, may involve one or more processes that are documented in the level-two procedures. Fifteen to twenty processes in the process map and ninety to one hundred processes in the level-two procedures manual, or a one-to-five relationship between processes in the process map and the subprocesses in the procedures manual, are recommended. For example, the business planning process may have the following procedures: customer expectations gathering, benchmarking, objectives setting and deployment, and business plan. (See figure 3.4 for a sample process map.)

THE IMPORTANCE OF COPS

COPs are not required by ISO/TS 16949, but are included in the IATF Quality Management Systems Assessment Check-List (also known as the IATF Checklist) and in IAOB auditor training as an approach to auditing processes. The IATF Checklist indicates that auditing ISO/TS 16949-conforming QMSs requires the auditing of COPs. COPs are defined in chapter 1 of the IATF Checklist as follows:

"The COP is a model that was introduced by ISO 9001:2000 and refers to the fact that any organization needs customer input to comply to specified and expected needs of the customer (output) in order to achieve customer satisfaction. This is accomplished by value adding processes of product realization and appropriate support processes, both enabled by management processes and provided resources."

Chapter 1 of the IATF Checklist also indicates that, " ...the auditor shall audit all applicable requirements to an identified COP." Figure 3.5 provides a representation of a COP as described by the IATF and the IATF Checklist. Only organizational processes that continuously repeat can meet customer requirements, so a series of processes, subprocesses, and support processes need to be defined by the organization and assessed by the auditor. Figure 3.6 presents a series of such processes, referred to as the octopus model, which is discussed during IATF training/qualification courses for third-party auditors.

Although not included in the IATF Checklist or the IATF Guidance to ISO/TS 16949:2002, at the ISO/TS 16949:2002 rollout meeting in May of 2002 the IATF provided examples of COPs, which include the following processes:

■ Market analysis
■ Bid/tender

Figure 3.5—A Customer-Oriented Process Model

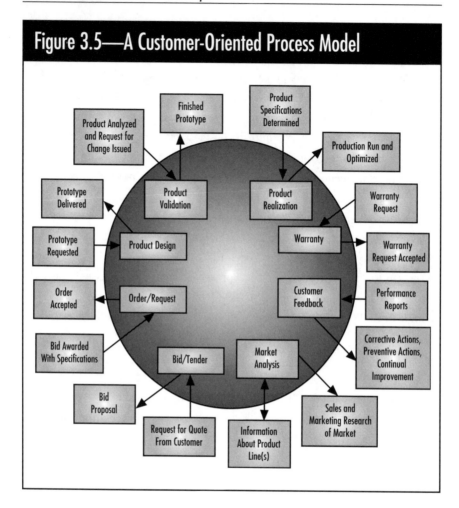

- Order/request
- Product and process verification/validation
- Product production
- Delivery
- Payment
- Warranty/service
- Post-sale/customer feedback

At the rollout meeting, the IATF also identified six "unique, but consistent" characteristics that are inherent in a process and necessary for an organization to have effective business/quality management:

■ A process owner exists.

■ The process is defined.

■ The process is documented.

■ Process linkages are established.

■ The process is monitored and improved.

■ Records are maintained.

Remember that the COP and the octopus model are not requirements for organizations implementing ISO/TS 16949. However, if an auditor requests documentation and other evidence relative to a COP, an organization is required to provide it. In reality, the auditor should be able to assess the COP by observing operations within an organization, which should demonstrate that these processes are implemented and effective. However, the creation of process maps, the defining of COPs, and iden-

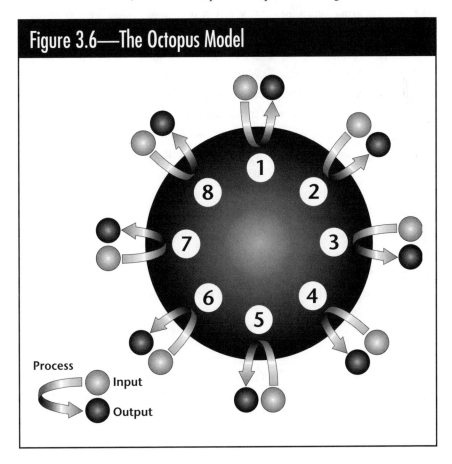

Figure 3.6—The Octopus Model

tification of process characteristics are the best implementation guidelines for the process approach. In addition, an existing methodology is available to help suppliers identify COPs, MOPs, and SOPs. It's referred to as the alignment methodology because it carefully aligns or links customer requirements that a supplier must satisfy to the supplier's quality objectives and to key processes that help meet customer requirements.

The methodology involves the use of an alignment chart to identify and list all the processes an organization uses to meet customer needs and expectations. The alignment chart supposes that most organizations have objectives and top management metrics. Creation of the alignment chart is a process of discovery, in which an organization aligns customer expectations, objectives, metrics, key processes, and process measurables. This process reveals whether strategic objectives support key customer expectations and whether metrics support strategic objectives.

The first step in this process is to identify customer expectations and group them into categories. Then the organization must identify the objectives that align with each customer expectation category. Next, the result measurables of the objectives must be identified. Result measurables show how well key processes work within the organization. The key to identifying processes is identifying the vital few key processes that influence the result measurables and help achieve customer expectations. For example, if "delivery" is a customer expectation, 100 percent on-time delivery is the strategic objective, and the result measurable is the percentage of on-time delivery. The key processes are maintenance, hiring, and manufacturing. The process measurables are percentage up-time, number of setup jobs vacant, and Cpk of machines. The alignment works like this: If machine up-time increases, so does percentage on-time, and that helps meet the customer expectation of on-time-delivery and the objective of 100 percent on-time delivery. The key processes in the alignment charts differentiate your organization from its competitors and help you fulfill customer needs and expectations. Key processes are the most important for the success of a business. Alignment chart methodology helps to identify key processes, which then need to be included in the process documentation in level two procedures. (See figure 3.7.)

The process list links the processes in the process map to level two procedures/processes. The process list also identifies process owners. The process list can be included in the business/quality manual along with the process map and

Figure 3.7—Alignment Chart

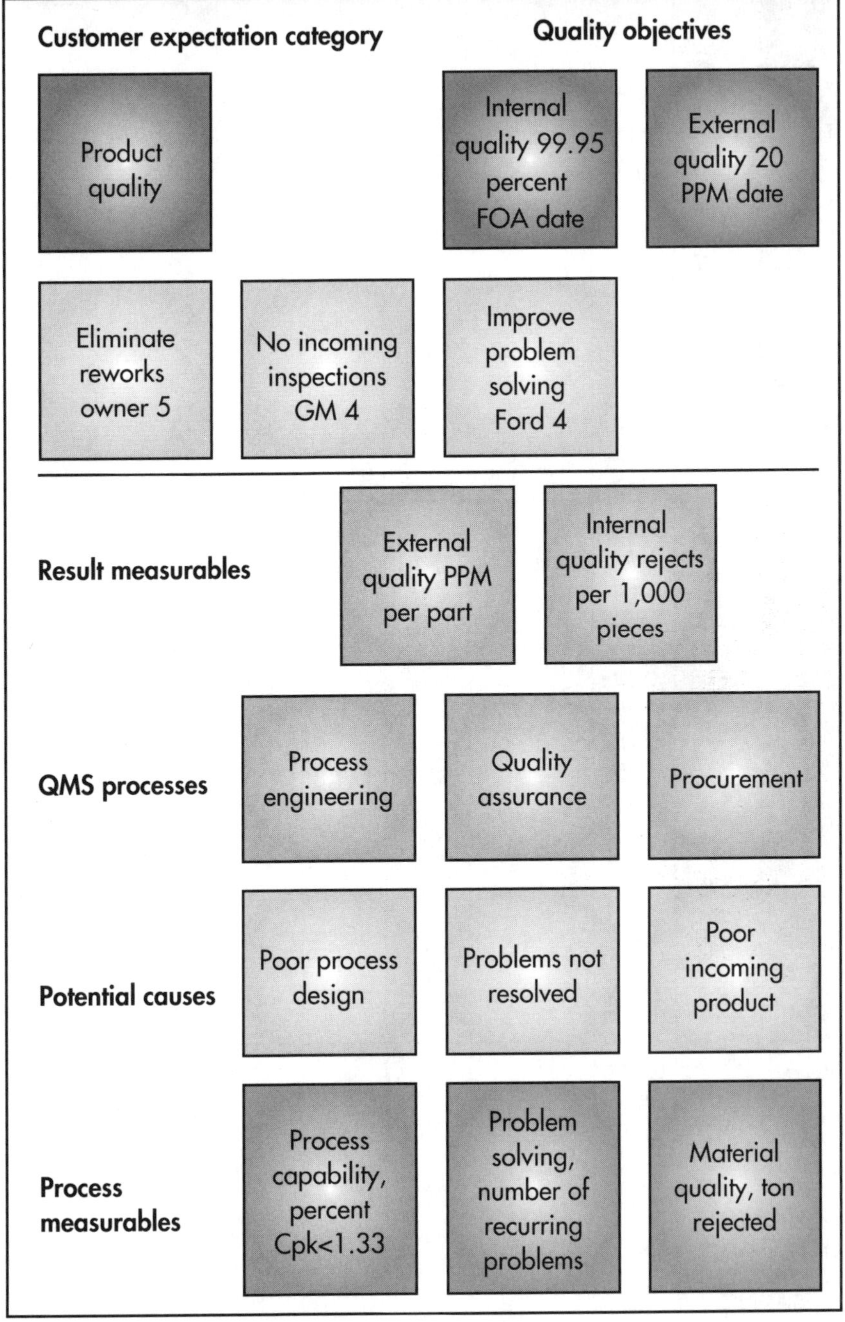

Customer expectation category

Quality objectives

Product quality	

Internal quality 99.95 percent FOA date	External quality 20 PPM date

Eliminate reworks owner 5	No incoming inspections GM 4	Improve problem solving Ford 4

Result measurables

External quality PPM per part	Internal quality rejects per 1,000 pieces

QMS processes

Process engineering	Quality assurance	Procurement

Potential causes

Poor process design	Problems not resolved	Poor incoming product

Process measurables

Process capability, percent Cpk<1.33	Problem solving, number of recurring problems	Material quality, ton rejected

Figure 3.8—Process List

Process	Subprocesses	Specification number	Customer-oriented process (C) or key process (K)	Owner (Title)
Design and development	Process FMEA	SOP 8-2501	(K) (C)	John Black
	Prototype development	SOP 8-2502	(K)	Jack Weed
	Mask development	SOP 8-2503		Gene Praschan

scope to satisfy the requirements of clause 4.2.2, Quality manual. (See figure 3.8 for a diagram of the process list.)

Finally, all of the processes in the map and certain level two procedures are listed in the business control plan. This plan ensures that business processes and process measurables are aligned to customer expectations. In other words, the business control plan documents the alignment chart but then goes on to do something even more important: identifying the acceptance level of each process metric and assigning responsibility for such measurement within the organization. It then goes on to identify how the process measurable is controlled (i.e., What is the mechanism of con-

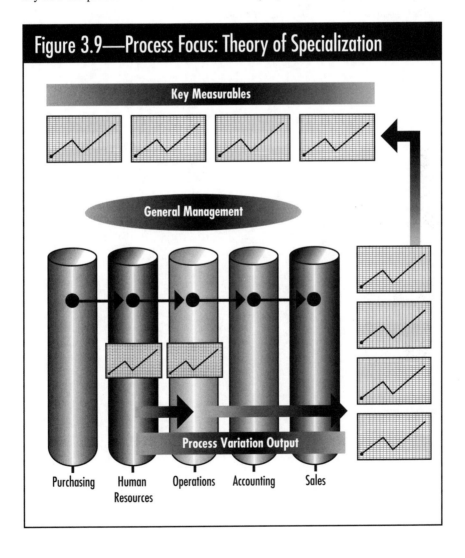

Figure 3.9—Process Focus: Theory of Specialization

trol?). Is it measured with management review, program management, a meeting, or measurement by a particular person? (See figure 3.8.)

Becoming process-focused is not easy. Moving from a hierarchical organization to a process-focused organization could indeed be the cost savings resulting from ISO/TS 16949. What are the cost savings? They are the realization that processes drive organizations and not departments. Today, we are overly department-focused, and merely measuring departmental effectiveness. ISO/TS 16949 and ISO 9001:2000 would rather have organizations focus on processes and measure their effectiveness and efficiency. Why? Processes drive results. (See figure 3.9.) These tools will be further discussed in the following chapters.

Chapter 4

Becoming Customer-Focused

B ecoming customer-focused is one of several key requirements to consider when transitioning from QS-9000 or ISO/TS 16949:1999 to ISO/TS 16949:2002. These key requirements are shown in appendix A. This chapter will explore clauses 5.2, 5.4, 5.6, and 8.2.1.

The key to understanding customer focus is to understand the linkages between clauses 5.2, Customer focus; 5.4, Planning; and 5.6, Management review. Also, the relationship between clauses 5.2, Customer focus, and 8.2.1, Customer satisfaction, should be understood.

Figure 4.1 shows the linkages between clauses 5.2, Customer focus, and 5.4, Planning. The objectives and the plan set in clause 5.4, Planning, need to be customer-focused. The organization needs to understand what the customer wants and set objectives related to customer expectations. Finally, figure 4.1 tells you that objectives are measured, reviewed, and improved in clause 5.6, Management review. Figure 4.2 explains the relationship between clauses 5.2, Customer focus, and 8.2.1, Customer satisfaction. Clause 5.2, Customer focus, requires that you listen to customer needs and expectations. Clause 8.2.1, Customer satisfaction, requires that you measure how happy customers are with the organization and is the output measure. Keep these requirements in mind as you read this chapter for more detailed explanations of these requirements.

5.2 CUSTOMER FOCUS

Most organizations that implement ISO/TS 16949 view customer expectations as an implementation afterthought rather than the first place to start. Customer expectations should affect an organization's strategy (including the objectives and

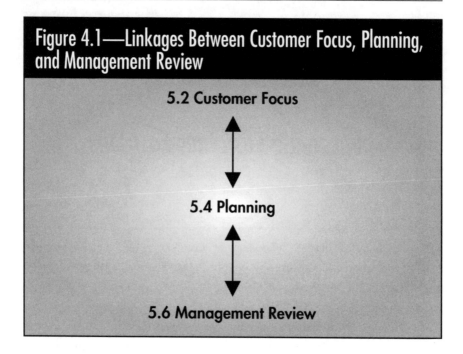

Figure 4.1—Linkages Between Customer Focus, Planning, and Management Review

5.2 Customer Focus

5.4 Planning

5.6 Management Review

business plan), and processes should be implemented that carry out the strategy. In practice, if an organization's processes are effective, then its strategy is driving the organization correctly and it will meet customer expectations. In this way a chain reaction can be seen between customer expectations, strategic objectives, the business plan, and processes designed to meet an organization's objectives.

Figure 4.3 illustrates how customer requirements, which are addressed in clause 5.2, are connected to other elements and activities of the quality management system (QMS) that are also found in ISO/TS 16949. Remember, as discussed in chapter 2, a QMS should be thought of as a business management system (BMS). If an organization understands that its management system must start with customer requirements, it will be able to implement a BMS that meets all of ISO/TS 16949's requirements because this will naturally follow from the business' operations. Furthermore, the BMS will make sense to employees because it follows the way processes naturally occur in the operation. This makes the management system easy to implement because it not only makes sense but it is also seen by everyone as having value, from top management to the sales representatives to the production line workers.

When determining which customer expectations need to be met, the implementation team will need to decide whether to look only at customers or to take an ISO

Figure 4.2—The Relationship Between Customer Focus and Customer Satisfaction

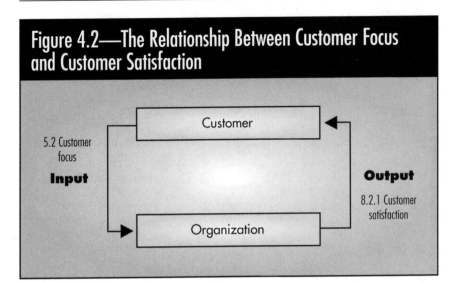

9004:2000 (or Malcolm Baldrige National Quality Award) view of interested parties. ISO 9000:2000 defines an interested party in clause 3.3.7 as a "person or group having an interest in the performance or success of an organization." An organization could consider some or all interested parties as customers with expectations to be met.

As the number of expectations grows or varies, what will be affected? Figure 4.3 should lead you to understand that your organization has to set objectives around expectations and then design processes that can deliver these expectations. The implementation team will look at the need to consider the expectations of interested parties in designing processes as additional "work," but some interested parties (e.g., community, employees, and suppliers) may play a key part in the organization's success. In some cases, these parties may be as strategically important to the business as the end customer. If parties other than customers have the potential to influence an organization's success (or even existence), the implementation team should include the expectations of all those interested parties when developing the BMS.

What follows is a methodology for relating customer expectations to organizational processes, strategic objectives, and process control methods. As outlined in table 4.2, this method can be used to align customer expectations with an organization's BMS activities. This table makes an excellent addition to a business/quality manual.

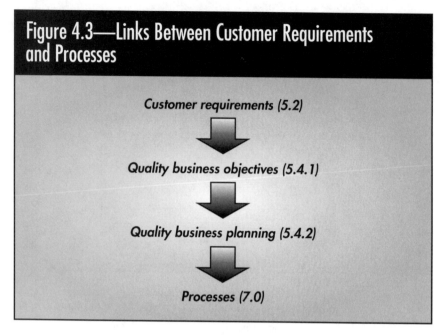

Figure 4.3—Links Between Customer Requirements and Processes

Customer requirements (5.2)

Quality business objectives (5.4.1)

Quality business planning (5.4.2)

Processes (7.0)

CUSTOMER EXPECTATIONS AND OBJECTIVES IN ISO/TS 16949

If you study clause 5.2, Customer focus, you'll discover that what it really says is, "Your organization needs to understand and be capable of satisfying customer requirements." Indeed, ISO/TS 16949 mentions customer requirements in many places. ISO 9000:2000 defines "requirement" in clause 3.1.2 as a "need or expectation that is stated, generally implied, or obligatory." With this definition, clause 5.2 requires your organization to understand and be capable of satisfying customer needs and expectations. If you look at clause 5.4.1.1, Quality objectives— Supplemental, you'll find that ISO/TS 16949 adds a note to ISO 9001:2000 that states, "Quality objectives should address customer expectations and be achievable within a defined time period."

There is an explicit intent in ISO/TS 16949 that expectations and objectives be aligned. Furthermore, clause 5.4.2, Quality management system planning, requires that top management ensure that, "The planning of the [QMS] is carried out in order to meet the requirements given in 4.1, as well as the quality objectives…"

The planning needs to not only address how the objectives are going to be met but also ensure that processes in the process map are implemented. To understand the linkage between clause 5.2 and section 7, Product realization (processes in the

Table 4.1—BMS Control Plan

Activity	Key Processes/ COPs	Customer Expectation	Measurable	Target Specification Reference	Control Monitoring Method
Manufacturing and Logistics	Order processing in production	Short cycle time	Cycle-time	20 Days	Monthly operations review
Manufacturing and Logistics	Manufacturing process	On-time delivery (OTD)	% OTD	100%	Weekly operations meeting

organization planned in clause 4.1, Quality management system—General require-ments, and clause 5.4.2), you need only to study the QMS process model on page x of ISO/TS 16949. Customer requirements are an input into an organization's processes (i.e., product realization and support processes), and the processes trans-late these inputs into product (which is an output). There is a linkage between what customers want (as determined in clause 5.2), the objectives set by the organization (as per clause 5.4.1), and the processes performed (as per section 7).

The only way organizations can ensure that they are capable of satisfying requirements is to translate a customer requirement into a process requirement for the organization. This expectation needs to be translated into a process measura-ble, as shown in table 4.2, and then measured and improved as required by clauses 4.1d, e, and f.

Becoming customer-focused means four things:

■ There is a process for customer/interested party needs and expectations that gathers and analyzes what customers want.

■ There is a matrix of customer needs and expectations linking objectives, processes, plans/projects, and management review (see table 4.3).

■ There is a BMS control plan (as shown in table 4.1) and an alignment chart (as shown in figure 3.8 in chapter 3). (These link customer focus and process focus).

■ The organization has updated the process list with processes that satisfy customer needs and expectations.

Accordingly, the last three of these activities need to be repeated each year when the business plan and budget are put together, using updated matrices and documents.

Customer Needs and Expectations Process

Every organization has multiple interactions with the customer. Sales interacts with purchasing at the customer. Top management interacts with the customer's top management. The quality organization interacts with the customer's quality organization. Shipping and logistics interact with the plant, and so on.

What are you learning from the customer? The process needs to take this information and process it. In other words, some of the information you need to process is short-term. Some of the information needs to become an input into the business strategy. For example, the customer may inform you that it is experiencing repeated problems with PPAPs not being submitted on time. It may also inform you that the organization is seeking suppliers with the most up-to-date XYZ technology. The problem with PPAPs not being submitted on time needs to be fixed immediately, with actions implemented in the short-term. In this case, at the very least, the information on the XYZ technology (and, for that matter, the PPAP timing) should be used in determining strategy. Best-in-class methods have suppliers making quarterly visits to their customers, where they can measure both expectations and satisfaction. This also allows them to give their customers information on what types of programs they have adopted to solve customer-related problems and to give them an update on customer-related key metrics. The customer's needs and expectations process can then describe what customer-related information can be applied to processes for both short-term and long-term actions. Processes can then be communicated to top management for inclusion in the business planning process.

5.4.1 QUALITY OBJECTIVES

Clause 5.4.1 requires that objectives or strategic goals be aligned with customer expectations (as shown in table 4.2). Although deemed quality objectives, these objectives extend beyond what is captured in any definition of product quality and can be referred to as business/quality objectives. Satisfying these business/quality objectives will ensure that the organization can meet customer/interested-party objectives. The addition of clause 5.4.1.1 in ISO/TS 16949 requires an automotive supplier to include quality objectives (and measurements of the

Table 4.2—Customer Needs and Expectations Matrix

Customer Expectation* (5.2)	Objectives (5.4.1)	Deployed Objectives/ Departments (5.4.1)	Related Processes (4.1. or 7.0)	Plan to Meet Objectives (5.4.2), including Resources (6.1)	Evidence of Objectives Being Met (5.6 or 8.5.1)

*Are you sampling product quality, delivery, technology, leadtime, reliability, cost, etc.?
*Note: Which dimensions are important to the customer?

achievement of those objectives) in its business plan, where they can address customer expectations.

Especially with the supplemental requirements in clause 5.4.1.1, customer expectations to be addressed by the objectives could include cost, lead time, delivery, and technology, along with product quality. Not only do these objectives need to be measurable, but they must also be deployed to relevant functions and levels within the organization. This means that the measurable objectives cannot just be high-level targets to be pursued and reviewed only by top management.

The organization will then need a deployment process to carefully assign responsibilities throughout the organization. Finally, these objectives need to be in the organization's business plan, as noted previously, which means that management throughout the organization must treat the quality objectives as part of the organization's business objectives.

In effect, there are three differences between ISO/TS 16949 and QS-9000 requirements when comparing clause 5.4.1 with QS-9000 clauses 4.1.1, Quality policy (in part), and 4.1.4, Business plan (in entirety). Although both require comprehensive objectives to be included in the business plan, ISO/TS 16949 also requires that they be:

■ Measurable

■ Deployed to relevant functions and levels within the organization

■ Aligned with customer expectations

The customer needs and expectations matrix links customer needs and expectations with objectives, deployed objectives, a plan/project to meet the objectives, and continual improvement/management review (clause 8.5.1/5.6), as shown in table 4.2.

The alignment chart and BMS control plan link customer focus and process focus. The alignment chart links customer expectations and objectives with key processes and process measurables. Again, customer expectations can only be met when processes ensure that they are met. If PPAP timing is important to the customer, then the PPAP process needs to measure the timing against customer deadlines.

5.4.2 QUALITY MANAGEMENT SYSTEM PLANNING

This section of ISO/TS 16949 is designed to ensure that there is a plan to meet the objectives detailed in the business plan (clause 5.4.1). In practical terms, this plan includes initiatives that are implemented by the organization to meet the objectives of its business plan. This helps the organization meet customers' needs and expectations. Additionally, for the plan to meet the objectives, the quality policy must be achieved. The plan also has to help the organization implement a process map or any changes to the processes in the process map. The plan must address the strategic implications to the BMS. Then it has to document the changes and address how the organization is going to cope with the change to the BMS.

5.6 MANAGEMENT REVIEW

The processes that constitute management review in ISO/TS 16949 are different from what was required by QS-9000. ISO/TS 16949 requires a form of management review that helps the organization become focused on improvement. Management review is spelled out in clause 4.1.3 of QS-9000. In this case, the review described sounds like a passive activity and was considered something of a quality system afterthought. Clause 5.6 of ISO/TS 16949 is quite different, requiring customer- and improvement-oriented meetings that help steer the business forward. Management review must now help identify and make changes to the quality policy, objectives, and the overall management system.

There are four aspects that differentiate management review in ISO/TS 16949 from what's found in QS-9000:

■ With ISO/TS 16949, management review includes analysis of twenty-one business categories. Table 4.3 identifies several clauses and other areas that require inclusion of topics (business categories) in the management review. Although there is some overlap between categories and some are more like individual measurements than full-fledged categories, they are classified as twenty-one categories to simplify the communication of the magnitude of the measurements required in management review.

■ Based on what is required in ISO/TS 16949, it's not practical to conduct this review in a single meeting once a year. In fact, treating all the categories that need to be reviewed on an equal basis will make management review difficult and unproductive. In reality, the top management team needs to consider the nature of the organization and decide the frequency with which each of the twenty-one categories needs to be subjected to evaluation and decision making. Some categories may require review on a monthly basis, while others may only need quarterly, semi-annual, or annual reviewing.

organization must proactively seek customer feedback and measure customer satisfaction. Indeed, accompanying the definition of customer satisfaction in clause 3.1.4 of ISO 9000:2000 are two notes that indicate an organization could be successful in meeting customer requirements for product quality and delivery, without having high "customer satisfaction perception." Your organization and its top management might want to treat these notes as a warning not to use proxy measures when determining customer satisfaction. Customer perception can only be gauged by asking the customer a variation of the question, "How satisfied are you with me?" In this manner, your organization can accurately measure the level of satisfaction with the various aspects of its relationship with the customer and better respond to customer needs as they affect satisfaction levels. A survey or interview is the only way to determine satisfaction, but the survey or interview must have value in terms of the information the organization obtains and must itself be a positive experience for the customer, one which does not lead to dissatisfaction.

ISO/TS 16949 requires a supplier to monitor the following four supplemental customer satisfaction measurements and improve them:

- Delivered part quality performance
- Customer disruptions (including field returns)
- Delivery schedule performance (including incidents of premium freight)
- Customer notifications related to quality or delivery issues

These measurements are considered the most basic metrics for determining customer satisfaction among automotive OEMs. The same measurements are required of suppliers. (See figure 7.4 in chapter 7.) Accordingly, they can become comprehensive measures of management system effectiveness within an organization and throughout the supply chain. Furthermore, ISO/TS 16949 states that after listing the customer satisfaction supplemental measures, "The organization shall monitor the performance of manufacturing processes to demonstrate compliance with customer requirements for product quality and efficiency of the process."

In other words, if the measurements are poor, there are no guarantees that processes aren't poor.

Both the requirement to measure customer perceptions and the requirement to measure supplemental customer satisfaction are new requirements to ISO/TS 16949:2002. These are not difficult measurements to make and use, nor is the measurement of customer perception a difficult new task that has no value. On the contrary, the OEMs are providing your organization with an opportunity to gain a better understanding of what is needed to satisfy the customer, thereby ensuring a better working relationship and creating potential opportunities for increased business.

Chapter 5

Design and Development, and Purchasing

wo of the biggest changes from QS-9000 to ISO/TS 16949 are in design and development, and in purchasing. In QS-9000, design and development meant only product design, but in ISO/TS 16949 it now also refers to process design. This significant change in design and development requires a structured methodology not only for product design but also for process design. Clause 7.3, Design and development, explores this change in more detail.

Purchasing has had two significant changes. The first change concerns the scope of purchasing; it now covers both products and services. The second change is the requirement for product suppliers of an ISO/TS 16949-registered organization to be ISO 9001:2000-registered.

This chapter will study design and development, as well as purchasing, in greater detail and explain the effect these requirements have on the transition from QS-9000 to ISO/TS 16949.

7.3 DESIGN AND DEVELOPMENT

The two most significant changes in clause 7.3 are the exclusion of advanced product quality planning (APQP) as a requirement and the inclusion of manufacturing process design as a new requirement. APQP was excluded because the International Automotive Task Force (IATF) is now made up of nine voting members, including several that have their own product-development processes. APQP remains a customer-specific requirement of DaimlerChrysler, Ford, and GM.

The inclusion of manufacturing process design input and output requirements (clauses 7.3.2.2 and 7.3.3.2) by the IATF is significant. QS-9000-compliant organizations will need to carefully study the requirements for process design in clause 7.3 and make the necessary changes to their new product development process. The real challenge comes when an organization actually has to implement these changes. In some QS-9000-registered organizations, the process engineering group, which is responsible for conformance, comprises only one or two people.

However, QS-9000-registered organizations shouldn't view this change negatively. When the first edition of QS-9000 was released in August 1994, the benefit to design-responsible organizations was a systematic design process. Many organizations went from chaotic product design to systematic design development. With ISO/TS 16949, one benefit will be a systematic method for manufacturing process design.

What are the challenges of incorporating manufacturing process design into a quality management system (QMS)? (As discussed in chapter 2, remember to think in terms of a business management system [BMS].) Although ISO/TS 16949 only specifies design input and output requirements, satisfying ISO/TS 16949's requirements in an effective manner will lead to the creation of a design-and-development plan that covers all phases of process design, including:

■ Manufacturing process design input
■ Manufacturing process design output
■ Design-and-development reviews
■ Monitoring of process design
■ Design-and-development verification
■ Validation of the manufacturing process

Organizations can decide whether to include process failure mode and effects analysis (PFMEA) as a verification process, and/or machine runoff as a validation process. One opportunity is to build mean time to repair (MTTR) and mean time between failures (MTBF) into the process design. Another is to build in an entire reliability and maintainability (R&M) methodology.

Leading-edge organizations already practice these processes and methodologies. An organization interested in the up-front involvement of its tooling and equipment suppliers can use the TE Supplement to QS-9000, which offers guidelines and specifies methodologies for PFMEA, machine runoff, R&M, MTTR, and MTBF for the entire life cycle of the manufacturing process.

Process design has been elevated to the same importance as product design in ISO/TS 16949. Both design of process and product now have the same type of expec-

Figure 5.1—APQP/AQP System Diagram

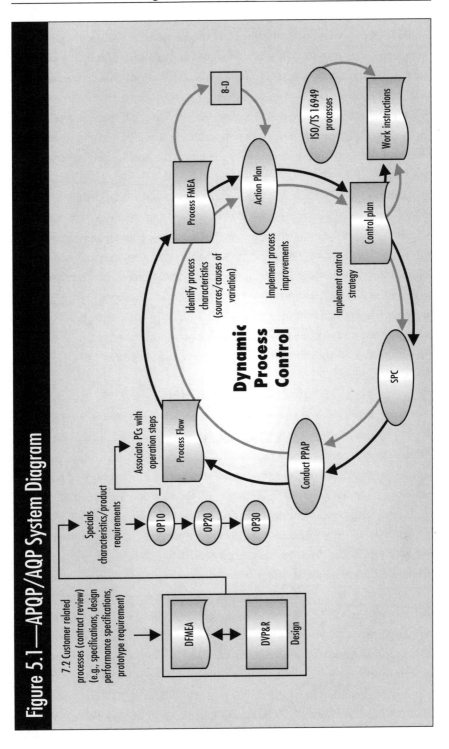

tations for inputs, outputs, verification, and validation. Tools such as design FMEA, special characteristics, design verification plan and report (DVP&R) (on the product design side), process flow, PFMEA, and control plans (on the process design side) need to be linked.

This is effectiveness in practice (i.e., the results that can be derived from implementing good product and process design practices). Think of it as preparing to take advantage of the coming economic upturn, when the most efficiently run operations will win.

Another requirement closely aligned with clause 7.3 is ISO/TS 16949's clause 8.2.3.1, Monitoring and measurement of manufacturing processes, which requires all new processes to be statistically studied. The closest point of comparison is the *Production Part Approval Process* manual, which only requires the study of processes with special characteristics. Many organizations will implement this requirement as the last step in the manufacturing process design and development phase. Design and development's change in scope with clause 7.3 (by including process design) requires both new documentation and subsequent implementation. However, if implemented properly, this new requirement can result in profits.

7.4 PURCHASING

The purchasing requirements haven't changed much from QS-9000. Organizations need to continue following their purchase order process (7.4.2, Purchasing information), supplier development process (7.4.1.2, Supplier quality management system development), and receiving inspection process (7.4.3, Verification of purchased product). What has changed is the scope of supplier development and the new requirement for supplier development that involves a registration deadline.

With ISO/TS 16949, there is no leeway on what constitutes a purchased product. Note 1 to clause 7.4.1, Purchasing process, defines purchased products as "all products and services that affect customer requirements…" Organizations are required to study their supplier lists and add all suppliers that affect customer needs and expectations, as per the previously mentioned ISO 9000:2000 definition of "requirement."

As for registration requirements, clause 7.4.1.2, Supplier quality management system development, calls for an organization conforming to ISO/TS 16949 to require its manufacturing suppliers to register "to ISO 9001:2000 by an accredited third-party certification body." The International Automotive Task Force (IATF) has

ISO/TS 16949:2002 FAQ—Supplier Development

IATF-communicated FAQs are clarifications of existing requirements. They are not new requirements, thus the original requirements should form the basis for reporting any noncompliance, not the FAQs.

Supplier Development (Revised July 2003. Answer reformatted for clarity)

Q: What are the requirements for supplier development clause 7.4.1.2?

A: ISO/TS 16949:2002 7.4.1.2 requires:

7.4.1.2, Supplier quality management system development

The organization shall perform supplier quality management system development with the goal of supplier conformity with this technical specification. Conformity with ISO 9001:2000 is the first step in achieving this goal.

Note: The prioritization of suppliers for development depends upon, for example, the supplier's quality performance and the importance of the product supplied.

Unless otherwise specified by the customer, suppliers to the organization shall be third-party registered to ISO 9001:2000 by an accredited third-party certification body.

IATF Guidance to ISO/TS 16949:2002 states:

7.4.1.2, Supplier quality management system development:

The burden is on the organization to demonstrate compliance of its suppliers to this requirement including evidence of alternative arrangements specified by the customer.

In situations where there are multiple customers, "customer approval" of alternative arrangements is based upon those customers impacted by that supplier.

"Supplier" in this clause (7.4.1.2) refers to sites where production and/or service parts specified by the customer are manufactured. See also the definition of "manufacturing," in clause 3.1.6.

Supplier quality management system development is the demonstrated performance of a process with the goal to achieve conformity with ISO/TS 16949:2002. Indicators of performance include:

- Conformity with ISO 9001:2000
- Achievement of ISO 9001:2000 certification, as a minimum, unless otherwise specified by the customer
- Compliance with ISO/TS 16949:2002, unless otherwise specified by the customer
- Evidence of a process to achieve the above steps

Supplier development was written purposely that way, with the provision that "unless otherwise agreed with the customer"—meaning—if not possible to do, get customer approval of a different approach. "Customer" in this context is defined in the guidance supplement as the "affected" customers. Also, guidance includes wording "a process to achieve the above"—meaning you could accept a plan to achieve the requirement—and as far as maximum timing of that plan, our view is that it should be achievable during the three year life of the certificate. Surveillance visits shall monitor achievement of the plan.

described this as meaning that suppliers need to be registered to ISO 9001:2000 within the first three years after the organization itself becomes ISO/TS 16949:2002-registered.

Although Note 2 to clause 7.4.1 indicates that a customer may "mandate alternative requirements" for subcontractors, this registration requirement is causing concern within tier-one suppliers and others trying to implement ISO/TS 16949. The IATF has explained that small "mom and pop" suppliers, "strategic" suppliers, or others that don't need to become ISO 9001:2000-registered can petition for waivers.

Other sources of information on supplier development are approved second-party audit schemes from Ford and GM, available in customer-specific requirements. Also, the International Automotive Oversight Bureau (IAOB) Web site contains a helpful discussion on the meaning of 7.4.1.2. (See figure 5.2.)

Please note that although the goal is supplier development to ISO/TS 16949, in all practicality the requirements are ISO 9001:2000 registration. See the FAQ. It remains to be seen whether this requirement will change in the future to ISO/TS 16949 conformance.

Chapter 6

Resources and Communication

Would you be worried if the pilot and co-pilot of an aircraft you were on couldn't communicate with the flight attendants, each other, or the control tower? Would you worry if the airline had no processes to ensure that aircraft maintenance and refueling were properly funded? Wouldn't you run for the exit door if you found out that the airline had no procedures for the selection and training of its pilots, flight attendants, mechanics, baggage handlers, and ticket agents?

These seem like absurd questions because it's difficult to imagine that an airline or any other organization would not have the capabilities and procedures for each of the issues mentioned. Yet, what guarantee do you have that the last business from whom you bought a product or service had similar capabilities and procedures? Three clauses in ISO 9001:2000 and ISO/TS 16949 contain new requirements that are a call for organizations, including automotive suppliers, to "look inward" so that they will be better able to meet or exceed customer needs and expectations. These three clauses are:

- 5.5.3, Internal communication
- 6.1, Provision of resources
- 6.2, Human resources

Specifying these requirements in clauses of a standard or technical specification may seem intrusive and excessive because they appear to be processes an organization could not function without anyway. However, from a common sense viewpoint, they are perfectly reasonable expectations. Unfortunately, companies routinely fail because they have substandard processes in place. Every organization should be doing what is required to meet customer specifications without interruption or difficulty, so specifying it in a standard or technical specification is simply a way for customers to have assurance that their suppliers are doing things in a practical way.

These three challenges represent those elements of your organization's business/quality management system (BMS) that ensure its processes are effective and efficient, and that your organization has the structures in place to support them. Although they don't directly involve interactions with the customer or the satisfaction of customer requirements, they do ensure that your system is able to provide an excellent product that ultimately satisfies customer requirements.

How should automotive suppliers approach these requirements? What new processes should they implement? What factors should they consider when implementing these requirements? In clause 6.2, there are some requirements spelled out for the first time, such as on-the-job training and employee motivation and empowerment. ISO/TS 16949 includes four more requirements than ISO 9001:2000 on this subject.

Questions most organizations should ask when they look at each of these three clauses (5.5.3, 6.1, and 6.2) are: Do we have an existing process that satisfies this requirement? Do we need to alter an existing process? Should we make a new process?

Examining these three inward-looking clauses represents an opportunity to review areas of the organization that are often imperfect and to produce greater internal (employee) and external (customer) satisfaction.

5.5.3 INTERNAL COMMUNICATION

As mentioned earlier, this is a new requirement to automotive suppliers. ISO/TS 16949 makes no changes to ISO 9001:2000's clause 5.5.3, which requires that "appropriate communication processes are established within the organization and that communication takes place regarding the effectiveness of the quality management system." Clause 5.5.3 is only one sentence long, but it has ramifications for requirements throughout ISO 9001:2000 and ISO/TS 16949, including many other requirements in section 5, Management responsibility, and clause 8.5.1, Continual improvement.

One of the goals of ISO Technical Committee 176 when it was creating ISO 9001:2000 was to increase the compatibility and alignment of its QMS requirements with the environmental management system (EMS) requirements contained in ISO

14001. Clause 5.5.3 is one of the changes in QMS requirements that increases alignment with ISO 14001's requirements. It's also a requirement that ties in with two of the eight quality management principles (involvement of people and continual improvement), which are the principles upon which ISO 9001:2000 is based.

"Involvement of People" states, "People at all levels are the essence of an organization, and their full involvement enables their abilities to be used for the organization's benefit." In effect, if an organization has a BMS conforming to clause 5.5.3, the resulting communication process will increase the involvement of people at all levels and make the system effective.

"Continual Improvement" states, "Continual improvement of the organization's overall performance should be a permanent objective of the organization."

Because the internal communication requirement concerns the effectiveness of the BMS, the goal of internal communication is not just to inform employees about the effectiveness of the BMS but also to help them understand what roles they play in the BMS and why they are important. Informing employees about how the BMS is operating plays a part in involving them and making them understand how they fit in.

The important question about internal communication is, "What information should be internally communicated?" An organization must establish processes for internal communication and communicate to employees the BMS' effectiveness. The organization must determine what internal processes provide results that show the effectiveness of the BMS. Organizations generally cite management review, internal audits, product conformity rates, customer satisfaction levels, and customer scorecards as processes or activities they use to measure the effectiveness of their BMS.

To be effective, clause 5.5.3 requires an internal communication process to analyze the results from these processes and facilitate decision making on what type of information is most suitable. Your organization also needs to determine what tools it will use for communication purposes. Communication tools include bulletin boards, e-mails, posters, flip-chart information, and the company newsletter.

As far as the content of these communications are concerned, the issue is whether a supplier's communication process should be restricted to the "effectiveness of the QMS," as required by ISO/TS 16949. This is an important issue for the automotive sector because many suppliers are required by one or more customers to obtain registration to ISO 14001. The same internal communication process may be used to satisfy ISO 14001's clause 4.4.3, Communication, which requires the organization, with regard to its environmental aspects and EMS, to "establish and maintain procedures for internal communication between the various levels and functions of the organization..."

The use of a single internal communication process for both EMS and QMS purposes avoids redundancy and increases systems integration. In addition, because an ISO 9001:2000-conforming BMS should be based on the process approach model, the process should not be limited to communicating the BMS' effectiveness. Top management should also use the internal communication process to communicate the importance of the customer as well as the legal requirements (as per clause 5.1a, Management commitment). Top management should also communicate the BMS responsibilities and authorities within the organization (clause 5.5.1) and could even use the process to ensure "the promotion of awareness of customer requirements throughout the organization" (clause 5.5.2c).

Many large suppliers that need to transition to ISO/TS 16949 have facilities scattered worldwide. These large organizations' workforces are multicultural and multilingual. Communications play an important part in making the employees understand that they are part of one organization with a shared vision, mission, quality policy, and quality objective. The business/quality manual is a good medium to communicate this information.

The quality manual is required by ISO 9001:2000 and not modified by ISO/TS 16949. It can be captured in one or two pages, including a scope statement, process map (or equivalent), and references to BMS processes/procedures and relevant business/quality documentation. Remember that quality is defined by how well the inherent characteristics of a product or process fulfill needs or expectations. For this reason, it's helpful to substitute the phrase "business management system" (BMS) for "QMS" when reading ISO 9001:2000 or ISO/TS 16949.

Can the business/quality manual play a role in communicating and creating a sense of unity among all of your organization's business processes? Remember that additional topics can be added to the business/quality manual, including mission and vision statements, the quality policy, customer expectations, quality and other objectives, plans to meet those objectives, and an organizational chart with responsibilities. The business/quality manual must be a living document that is updated yearly and helps communicate key aspects of the BMS, including strategy and continual improvement projects.

6.1 PROVISION OF RESOURCES

Clause 6.1 can be described as the resource allocation process that determines and provides the resources to implement and maintain the BMS. Resources are also needed for continual improvement (of BMS effectiveness) and to increase customer satisfaction. For the automotive supplier that wants to remain competitive, satisfying clause 6.1 represents an opportunity to establish processes for determining the resources needed for other business processes as well. Most suppliers implementing ISO/TS 16949 can consider the budgeting and project justification processes as satisfying the requirements of clause 6.1. However, do these processes consider customer satisfaction or the effectiveness of the BMS when allocating resources? This is important to address if the QMS is to be a BMS, because most allocation processes in organizations consider cost justification. In addition, the supplier will need to determine if these resource provision processes allow for BMS effectiveness and customer satisfaction.

In reality, the allocation of resources is directly or indirectly cited in several ISO/TS 16949 clauses outside clause 6.1:

- Clause 5.4.2, Quality management system planning, requires the organization to plan to meet the quality objectives and implement and maintain the processes designed to conform to the requirements of clause 4.1. All of this planning will require resources to be executed in order. The requirements of clause 5.4.2 may be incorporated into the organization's business planning process where objectives are set and a yearly budget is prepared.

- Clause 5.6, Management review, requires the top management team to discuss the opportunities for BMS improvement and then make resource allocation decisions in line with the requirements of clause 5.6.3, Review output.

- Clause 6.2, Human resources, requires the organization to provide training or take other actions to ensure employee competency. This means that the organization will need to allocate resources to ensure the availability of employees competent for each task.

- Clause 6.3, Infrastructure, and 6.4, Work environment, also require resources for maintenance and improvement. Ongoing maintenance of infrastructure and work environment may be in the process. Capital expenditures, however, are probably planned when the budget is prepared. (See clause 5.4.2.)

There are other requirements in ISO/TS 16949 that require a supplier to provide resources to ensure that the organization can meet the requirements of the customer and ISO/TS 16949. Although clause 6.1 clearly states that all these areas need to be provided for, it is easy to limit the scope of processes in the BMS to those necessary for implementation and maintenance of the BMS structure (e.g., implementation team and auditing expenses).

For example, to satisfy clause 7.1, Planning of product realization, you will need to determine the required resources specific to the product, particularly for new product development, and this will involve advanced product quality planning, phase I. Clause 7.3.1, Design and development planning, requires detailed plans for design and development of product, and the plans must include the resources required to make the plans useful to business activities and meeting customer requirements.

Finally, clause 8.4, Analysis of data, requires suppliers to identify the most suitable opportunities for continual improvement. This requirement connects with clause 8.5, Improvement, which, in turn, requires suppliers to carry out those improvements. What a true businessperson will always want to know up front is how much these activities and opportunities will cost and what must be provided if the organization is to meet customer requirements and gain long-term improvements. "Provision of Resources" could also be titled "BMS Investment Process."

In this way, clause 6.1 shows up directly and indirectly in many places throughout ISO/TS 16949. Fortunately, the resource allocation process need not cite every instance where it is used. Instead, the processes using resource allocation can cite the provision of resources process as a reference.

6.2 HUMAN RESOURCES

Clause 6.2 requires that personnel performing work affecting product quality must be "competent." The first determination that an automotive supplier must make is who in the organization affects product quality. Automotive suppliers, especially suppliers to Ford Motor Co., should know the answer to this question by now because it was asked in Ford's Q-101 requirements. Of course, the answer is everyone in the organization. To conform with the requirements of clause 6.2 in ISO 9001:2000 and ISO/TS 16949, an organization must have a process to determine the competency of personnel (including everyone from top management to machine operators) and whether personnel in particular positions demonstrate required capabilities.

This is new to QS-9000-registered suppliers, which previously used a training plan. Detailed training plans and effective training programs are not enough to ensure competency. Training by itself is not enough.

Many suppliers use their job appraisal process to determine the competency required of the employee(s) doing a given job. To be effective, the appraisal process must identify factors specific to the job being performed by an employee (e.g., skills and experience). The supervisor can then rate how well the employee has performed in the factors specified on the appraisal form.

However, be aware that there is typically a problem with using U.S. appraisals in other countries because of confidentiality laws prohibiting the sharing of appraisal information. Organizations circumvent this legal requirement by getting the approval of the persons involved and/or by not showing the registrar's auditor an actual employee rating on the appraisal form. In effect, the supervisor could rate employee performance/potential performance for the factors but not put the rating in writing, where others might see this confidential information. Other organizations use a skills matrix along with a training plan. However, the bottom line is that every employee who affects quality needs to be evaluated to see if he or she satisfies the competency requirements for the job. Clause 6.2.2 requires that if an employee is not competent to perform a job, the organization must provide training or take some other action to remedy the deficiency. The organization must also evaluate whether the actions taken were effective.

This is a departure from QS-9000, which only required that organizations understand the effectiveness of training taken. Here are two suggestions for evaluating the effectiveness of the actions taken:

- *Establish an appraisal system identifying the effectiveness of the actions taken.* In other words, the supervisor would document whether training, working with another person, or a change in job function produced the desired results. This looks specifically at employee competency.

- *Relate the effectiveness of the actions taken to an associated improvement in the area, in a related process, or in a measurable that is capable of being documented.* Rather than evaluating the actions themselves or employee competence independently of all other things, the effectiveness of the actions taken will be determined by looking at the changes those actions have produced within the organization. In reality, the goal is to ensure that employees are capable of performing processes effectively so that customer requirements are met and/or exceeded. Rather than just measuring employee competency, you are measuring the competency of the process(es) after actions have been taken.

Other new requirements in clause 6.2.2 are the need for employees to understand the relevance and importance of their activities and their overall contributions toward business/quality objectives, from systemwide objectives to individual employee goals. This requirement relates back to the quality management principle of promoting the involvement of people in the organization. When personnel understand their importance and overall benefit to the organization, they will become more involved in the continual improvement of the BMS and the organization. This should ultimately increase employee satisfaction. In fact, of the three clauses this chapter has explored, ISO/TS 16949 adds requirements only to clause 6.2.2, by including 6.2.2.4, which requires the organization to measure employee awareness.

FOUR SUPPLEMENTAL REQUIREMENTS IN 6.2.2

ISO/TS 16949 adds four requirements to clause 6.2.2 that emphasize the importance of personnel in affecting the organization's ability to meet customer requirements. These requirements, although certainly applicable to any organization in any sector, are considered critical by the automotive OEMs. We will briefly examine what, if anything, automotive suppliers need to do to satisfy these added requirements.

6.2.2.1 Product Design Skills

The requirements in 6.2.2.1 are not new to automotive suppliers. This clause specifies that organizations need to ensure that those involved in product design have the competency and design tool and technical skills necessary to effectively engage in product design. Also, the required tools and techniques for design activity must be identified. QS-9000-registered suppliers have already had to focus on basics, such as geometric dimensioning and tolerancing, design failure mode and effects analysis, problem solving, and design of experiments. The difference is more a matter of ensuring that individual employees have suitable competency to participate in the design processes. In other words, if the design group is required to perform these tasks, the design skills matrix needs to reflect these tasks and the tools and techniques required. Then the supplier can evaluate employee competency in this critical activity.

6.2.2.2 Training

This clause requires documentation of the organization's training needs. These requirements can be documented in an annual training plan. This clause also discusses the need to qualify personnel with an "emphasis on customer-specific requirements." Qualification differs from competency. Competency can be measured by an appraisal, but does not indicate whether the employee is qualified to perform the job. There is also an emphasis on customer-specific requirements in ISO/TS 16949 by virtue of the sheer number of customer-specific requirements at present. It's important to remember that the number of OEM subscribers to ISO/TS 16949 is higher than for QS-9000. Also, in reality, the customer-specific requirements were not given their due importance in QS-9000. Suppliers now need to create a link between customer-specific requirements and contract review procedures. This linkage must be documented in the training process and implanted in a training plan. All the other requirements in 6.2.2.2 are the same as those in QS-9000.

6.2.2.3 Training on the Job

This is a new requirement not contained in QS-9000. Most organizations readily acknowledge that the most important training they perform is the on-the-job training of their personnel. Consequently, you will need to ensure that on-the-job training is identified in the training matrix and treated as a BMS requirement that needs to be fulfilled. Be sure to have a training record when this requirement is fulfilled. Clause 6.2.2.3 also contains another requirement: Personnel whose work affects quality must be informed about the consequences to the customer of nonconformity to business/quality requirements.

Although this requirement is new to QS-9000-registered suppliers, it's not a difficult one to satisfy and can be easily fulfilled by an FMEA document. In the typical FMEA form, the "Effects of the Failure" column already describes the consequence of a quality requirement nonconformity. If the FMEA has been completed with documentation of the special characteristics' failure modes, this may be a good document to use for on-the-job training purposes. The operator could also use the FMEA to respond to questions regarding 6.2.2.3 during an audit.

6.2.2.4 Employee Motivation and Empowerment

This requirement is derived from VDA 6.1, the German automotive OEM BMS requirements that were based on ISO 9004-1:1994, and it will be new to QS-9000-

registered suppliers. Clause 6.2.2.4 requires the supplier to have a process to moti-
vate employees to achieve objectives and to empower them to identify and make
continual improvements to the BMS. The process should also promote innovation
and awareness of quality and technological innovations and opportunities. Elements
that a supplier could adopt for this process include employee surveys, award programs, and improvement suggestion processes, all of which can be used to moti-
vate and empower employees. Additionally, clause 6.2.2.4 asks the organization to
have a process that will be used to "measure the extent to which its personnel are
aware of the relevance and importance of their activities…" One simple way to satisfy this requirement is for a supplier to audit this awareness during internal and
process audits. Using this method, the organization can measure and track the percentage of personnel aware of the importance and relevance of their contributions
to organizational success.

SUMMARY

Clause 5.5.3, 6.1, and 6.2 contain requirements that can result in many changes
within the typical supplier organization that has only done the bare minimum to obtain
QS-9000 compliance and registration in the past. Organizations that have an effective BMS, which not only satisfies the requirements of QS-9000 but also has systems to meet the internal and external organizational needs, may already be in
conformity with many of ISO/TS 16949's newer requirements. However, every supplier will need to study the new requirements, identify gaps that need to be filled
and existing processes that need to be modified, and then implement/alter processes
as needed to satisfy ISO/TS 16949's requirements.

These three ISO/TS 16949 clauses share a common element mentioned earlier:
They stress the importance of having processes that enable your organization and
its employees to meet the needs of your customers, whether they are OEMs, tier-
one suppliers, or others. Indeed, most of the seventeen key challenges that are covered in this series are clauses that contain BMS requirements which do not exist "in
a silo," but rather specify processes that will interact with many other processes. It's
impossible to make the transition to ISO/TS 16949:2002 by implementing all the
new and altered processes and considering every interaction involved; however, look
for connections in the process flow and revise the BMS to reflect the flow of activities within your facilities.

You may work for an organization that already knows that the OEMs have set mandates for ISO/TS 16949 registration or knows that your customers and the nature of your organization make ISO 9001:2000 with ISO/TS 16949 compliance the likely requirement. Some tier-two suppliers are not yet sure whether registration or compliance with ISO/TS 16949 will be the requirement. Whatever your organization's status, what is discussed above and in previous chapters will apply to your organization if your organization supplies the automotive sector.

Chapter 7

Control, Measure, and Analyze

The last few differences between ISO/TS 16949:2002 and QS-9000 are covered in this chapter. Each of these topics is important in its own right. The differences are:

- Clause 7.1.4, Change control
- Clause 8.2.2, Internal audit
- Clause 8.2.3, Monitoring and measurement of processes
- Clause 8.4, Analysis of data

The most important of these differences may be internal auditing. The International Automotive Task Force (IATF) considers process auditing the key difference between QS-9000 and ISO/TS 16949.

Change control, though not a new topic for the automotive industry, has become an important topic for many tier-one suppliers. If this requirement is not properly implemented, it will hinder many internal processes, including continual improvement. Internal auditing has gained importance and provoked much discussion in the automotive industry. This is mainly a result of IATF's assertion that process auditing is the key difference between QS-9000 and ISO/TS 16949 auditing practices. The IATF has also said to "throw away the checklist" in an effort to de-emphasize the importance of a checklist mentality and to focus attention on the process that is being audited.

This chapter will discuss how the audit process has changed from QS-9000 to ISO/TS 16949. In the section on clause 8.2.3, Monitoring and measurement of processes, we'll reintroduce the business management system (BMS) control plan. This document and the manufacturing control plan lay out the overall control strategy for the entire business, including manufacturing and nonmanufacturing processes. Clause 8.4, Analysis of data, will also be discussed. This section also examines methods to reduce costs.

7.1.4 CHANGE CONTROL

Although QS-9000 contains clause 4.9.5, Process changes, QS-9000 does not require an organization to "have a process to control and react to changes that impact product realization" to the extent that ISO/TS 16949 does. In fact, something approaching this requirement was contained in the last edition of Ford's Q-101. In that edition, which preceded QS-9000, question three of the Ford Quality Assessment proposed the need for change control or managing change, along with a checklist on how to manage the change. The "manage the change" process introduced in the last edition of Q-101 included a checklist that considered a long list of design, manufacturing, and business/quality documents that could be affected when a change was implemented.

The reason that this requirement was included in the Q-101 Quality Assessment was to measure ways in which changes caused shutdowns on supplier assembly lines or in the organization's own facilities. Typical examples include:

- A coolant change in a manufacturing process interacts with the coolant in a washer, either in the organization's own facility or at the assembly plant.
- A design change in a component interacts negatively in the assembly or subassembly of the product.

Change control, as defined in clause 7.1.4, is linked directly to the production part approval process (PPAP). In effect, product or process changes that affect product realization need to be evaluated and verified by the organization. The customer should be apprised of any change, as defined in the related PPAP reference manual, including changes to the customer's proprietary designs. If a PPAP is required, it should be conducted to confirm that the change had no effect on the ability of the product and/or process to meet customer specifications. Of course, PPAP is only a customer-specific requirement of DaimlerChrysler, Ford, and GM. The customer-specific requirements of your organization's individual customer(s) need to be considered when conforming with change control.

Although clause 7.1.4 is a new requirement in ISO/TS 16949:2002, it's not really new to the U.S. automotive industry. This requirement was included by most organizations during QS-9000 implementation, either because of PPAP or Q-101.

The biggest effect of clause 7.1.4 can be found in this statement: "For proprietary designs, impact on form, fit, or function... shall be reviewed with the customer..." This requirement differs slightly from QS-9000, where clause 4.4.9.1, Design changes—Supplemental, required that "impact on form, fit, function, performance, and/or durability shall be determined with the customer so that all effects can be properly evaluated."

The expectation is that the organization is now responsible for considering the effect of changes both on customer-owned design and the designs that the organization owns. Involving proprietary designs in change control was an approach not implemented in many of the large tier-one automotive suppliers registered to QS-9000. Now, even though the design is proprietary, changes affecting form, fit, or function need to be evaluated with the customer. This can enhance customer-supplier relations in some cases.

One large tier-one supplier that has hundreds of factories worldwide is rolling out a "manage the change" process across several business units. The reason for the rollout is that changes in products and/or processes are causing severe problems for its OEM customer. The organization promised the customer that it would roll out a worldwide program and is now in the process of doing that, using considerable resources and time.

Reviewing the existing change process has clarified several factors this organization needs to consider, including:

- What types of changes need to be included in the process?
- Should all changes go through this process, including document changes?
- How centralized or decentralized should this process be? (Centralization provides for more control, but it results in less speed in making changes.)
- How many people should be involved in the change process? (More people may mean less risk but can result in less speed and more cost.)

For this organization, this implementation effort clarified the importance of managing the change process in regard to the customer, the quality of the product, and the organization. Most organizations would be wise to study and implement this process carefully as they revise their business/quality management systems (BMSs) to satisfy clause 7.1.4.

8.2.2 INTERNAL AUDIT

Internal audits are required by ISO/TS 16949:2002 to "check" (in the plan-do-check-act cycle) whether the organization is truly meeting all of the requirements of its own BMS and ISO/TS 16949, which requires three types of audits: quality system audits, process audits, and product audits. The intent of ISO/TS 16949 and the similarities and differences between each of these audits is presented below.

Quality System Audit

The intent of this audit is to ascertain whether the overall system is effective and efficient. This is a formal audit that needs to be conducted in the same way as an external audit. In this audit, the auditors ensure that the organization is moving toward its goals and objectives and that the customer satisfaction and supplemental customer satisfaction metrics are being satisfied.

Audit planning is key in the quality system audit trail. We've already discussed the need to audit processes rather than clauses. The process approach recommends using operational customer complaints and management review data to identify processes that need to be included in the audit plan. The turtle diagram helps the auditor determine additional processes that need to be sampled.

Good auditors look for three items: intent, effective implementation, and effectiveness in practice. Intent refers to whether an organization properly interpreted the standard and has translated the proper intent into its processes. Effective implementation means that the documentation has been implemented as planned (i.e., whether the organization is doing what it says it is doing). Effectiveness in practice analyzes whether the organization is implementing the process as planned and getting the results from the implementation. (Is the process delivering? Is the organization delivering?)

Internal auditors can look for effective implementation and effectiveness in practice. Effective implementation checks the process against the process documentation. In ISO/TS 16949, the internal auditor must check these process characteristics:

- A process owner exists.
- The process is defined.
- The process is documented.
- Process linkages are established.
- The process is monitored and improved.
- Records are maintained.

Examine the records (i.e., objective evidence) generated by the process over time. Do the records show that the process is being followed? Follow the audit trail of the process using the turtle analysis and standard audit linkages. Also, it's critical to choose the right samples when following the audit trail. The samples shown in the audit trail in figure 7.1 were new products that recently underwent PPAP, products that were released a few months ago, and/or new products still in the pipeline. With this method, the process can be audited in three different timeframes.

Process Audit

ISO/TS 16949 requires that each manufacturing process be audited. How does this audit differ from the quality system audit? The quality system audit is able to assess the overall system performance and the system's effectiveness in meeting organizational goals and objectives. The process audit takes a comprehensive look into how each process actually works. This examination takes place at a work instruction level. The auditor should start with customer complaints, rework, scrap, and Cpk data within the manufacturing process and begin sampling the operations to audit the process flow.

A process flow, PFMEA, and control plan should be used during this audit. This audit should ensure that weeks of data generated from the process are sampled retroactively. This audit should also sample all of the pertinent elements from the plant floor. The audit should not be clause-focused but process-focused.

When auditing the process, the following areas should be sampled:

■ Work instructions and the operator's knowledge of them
■ Inspections carried out against the control plan (check weeks of data retroactively)
■ Calibration of the gages/tests
■ SPC charting and out-of-control conditions
■ Operator's knowledge of what he or she is charting
■ Nonconforming material and how it is handled
■ How nonconforming material is reported
■ How information is collected for cost of poor quality
■ Operator preventive maintenance
■ Product identification and traceability (if applicable)
■ Housekeeping
■ Verification of changeovers and new setups
■ How inventory is stored and amount of inventory (FIFO and LIFO

Figure 7.1—New Product Development Audit Trail

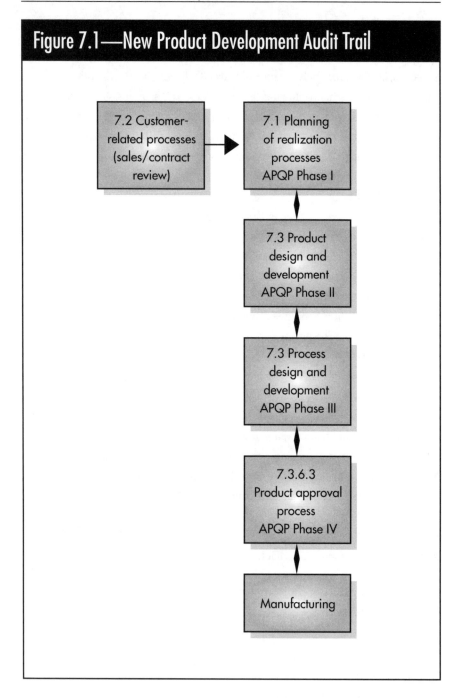

When auditing the plant floor, process linkages may take the auditor to many other areas of the plant, including training/competency, gage lab (calibration/MSA), and purchasing (for materials purchased in department).

When ISO/TS 16949 processes become mature, why not expand the process audit from only manufacturing processes to all the processes in the process map? The process audit can examine in detail whether the process goals and objectives are being accomplished in an organization.

Product Audits

The intent of the product audit is to verify the control plan's controls in different stages of production, including at the shipping dock. The process audit verifies that the process is being followed, whereas the product audit verifies that the control plan is being followed. Many years ago, this verification was the job of the inspector, who would randomly sample products to confirm that the operator was indeed doing the necessary inspection.

The product audit asks how the organization knows if the product checks, as required by the control plan, are being carried out. Organizations need to sample products and manufacturing processes, including the dock, to ensure that the product dimensions, functionality, packaging, and labeling are indeed occurring as planned.

Auditor Training

It's important that the personnel conducting both system audits and process audits be trained auditors. They should attend a formal auditing course that teaches audit planning using customer-oriented processes (COPs), turtle analysis, and audit trails. It's also important for auditors to understand the overall auditing process, including conducting opening meetings, writing nonconformances, and conducting closing meetings. Most important, auditors need to understand how to close out nonconformances. Registrar Accreditation Board-certified internal or lead auditor courses typically teach the auditing process as required by ISO 19011. Currently, this is only a requirement of GM's customer-specific requirements for auditors.

With internal auditing, the biggest difference between QS-9000 and ISO/TS 16949 is that QS-9000 does not specify system or process audits. Clause 4.17 of QS-9000 only requires internal audits to be performed (in accordance with Appendix B, Code of Practice for Quality System Certification Bodies/Registrars) that cover all the elements of QS-9000. ISO/TS 16949 is more specific and requires system and product audits on top of process audits. The internal system audits need to evaluate the processes in the organization, including COPs and their support processes. The product audits in ISO/TS 16949 must verify conformance to product dimensions (requirements in the manufacturing processes), while the process audits must assess the manufacturing processes for conformity with defined procedures and customer specifications. Clause 8.2.2 of ISO/TS 16949:2002 is an important requirement that can drive BMS improvement. Experience has shown that third-party registrar/auditor requirements tend to flow down into the organizations being audited, thereby affecting internal audits.

Internal audits should verify that the BMS conforms to ISO/TS 16949, meets customer and organizational needs and expectations, and identifies opportunities for continual improvement of the system and processes. However, registrar auditors will examine your organization's internal audit program to ensure that it meets the requirements of clause 8.2.2 and does so to the expectations of the OEMs subscribing to ISO/TS 16949. OEMs that are members of the IATF have issued comments on registrar auditing, based to a large degree on their observations of registrar audits of automotive suppliers for conformity with ISO/TS 16949 during an IATF pilot registration program in February of 2002. Based on the registrar audits IATF witnessed, it's worth examining problems, need for improvement in auditing practices, and the key differences between QS-9000 and ISO/TS 16949 as you begin to evaluate and revise your internal audit program.

The sidebar on page 91 presents a summation of IATF comments at an April 2002 ISO/TS 16949:2002 rollout meeting regarding new concepts on how auditing is to be conducted with ISO/TS 16949. This summation also provides an overview of the gaps that the IATF identified while observing pilot registration assessments of automotive suppliers to ISO/TS 16949:2002.

8.2.3 MONITORING AND MEASUREMENT OF PROCESSES

The requirements in clause 8.2.3 apply to both manufacturing and nonmanufacturing processes. For manufacturing processes, the monitoring and measurement defined in the manufacturing control plan should have been completed by the organization during the new product development launch process.

Summation of IATF Comments on Registrar Auditing and Gaps Found in Pilot

Auditing ISO/TS 16949:2002—Key Approach Differences as Viewed by the IATF:

- Process Approach to Audit. Customer-Oriented Processes. These processes start with customer requirements and end with output going back to the customer. The input and output need to be checked against each other to see if the output satisfies the input. IATF wants all the COPs identified in the organization. IATF wants the process to have a clear line of sight from the customer to the organization.
- The audit plan should have key processes instead of just clauses. The plan needs to identify the key processes.
- Performance. Linked to common metrics for the organization and its suppliers (as per clause 8.2.1.1 Customer satisfaction—Supplemental, and 7.4.3.2 Supplier monitoring)
- Oversight—Adherence to the ISO/TS 16949:2002 registration scheme "rules" and common global oversight body process
- An organization needs to throw away the checklist and use its procedure to do the internal audit. Use the checklist to make sure your organization is thorough but not as the definitive list of what the QMS must do to conform with ISO/TS 16949:2002.
- The IATF stressed the problem of remote locations not being able to get stand-alone certificates
- To obtain ISO/TS 16949:2002 certificates of registration, sites must be automotive production and service parts suppliers
- Each OEM will have a link to its Web site where the customer-specific requirements documentation can be obtained.

Gaps Found During Pilot ISO/TS 16949:2002 Registrar Audits:

- Control plans were poor and not followed
- Customer specifics ignored
- Registration scheme rules not followed
- Internal auditor training was poor
- Records not linked to procedure
- On-the-job training not addressed
- Unreported changes (production part approval process or PPAP)
- Management never audited
- Interface between site and remote location not followed
- PPAP did not meet requirements
- GR&R (gage repeatability and reproducibility) performed by calibration technicians and not production operators
- Written findings did not have three elements: requirement, objective evidence, and nature of nonconformance

The measurement and improvement of nonmanufacturing processes will be new to QS-9000-registered organizations. Clause 4.1, Quality management system—General requirements, requires an organization to "monitor, measure, and analyze these processes [needed for the BMS], and implement actions necessary to achieve planned results and continual improvement of these processes." Clause 8.2.3 also requires that all processes be monitored and measured to "demonstrate the ability of the processes to achieve planned results."

Organizations should use a business management system (BMS) control plan to plan for and control nonmanufacturing processes. Figure 7.2 provides an example from a BMS control plan. A complete version of this would list all processes from the process map, including customer-, management- and support-oriented processes (COPs, MOPs, and SOPs). Control methods, along with customer expectations affecting these processes, measurements, and acceptance criteria, are listed in the BMS control plan.

Control methods can include individual and/or team meetings that review the measurables. Through such meetings, an organization can clearly delegate responsibility and achieve the desired result of clause 8.2.3: fulfillment of product and process specifications, BMS goals, and objectives.

In addition to the ISO 9001:2000 requirements, the IATF included two additional related requirements when drafting ISO/TS 16949:

■ Process studies for new manufacturing processes
■ Ongoing process capability

These requirements are contained in clause 8.2.3.1, Monitoring and measurement of manufacturing processes.

The requirements in conducting process studies for new manufacturing processes can be found in the customer-specific requirements for PPAP, written by DaimlerChrysler, Ford, GM, and other OEMs having such requirements. However, clause 8.2.3.1 also requires that process studies be conducted every time a new manufacturing process is introduced into the organization. When the manufacturing process study is conducted, production specifications and objectives for manufacturing process capability, reliability, maintainability, and availability must be documented. This requirement parallels what is found in clause 7.3.3.2, Manufacturing process design output, as is appropriate. An organization can follow the same process for design and development of manufacturing processes when it introduces a new manufacturing process.

The second requirement contained in clause 8.2.3.1 that warrants examination is an ongoing process capability requirement. ISO/TS 16949 specifies that the manufacturing process needs to maintain the process capability or performance that it had when it obtained initial product approval, but on an ongoing basis. For organizations using PPAP, a Ppk 1.67 was required for initial product approval. This means that an organization using PPAP must consistently maintain a Ppk 1.67.

8.4 ANALYSIS OF DATA

Clause 8.4 requires that an organization not only collect data about its processes and product but that it also use that data to make decisions about the BMS. Data must be collected and analyzed to provide the organization with four types of information:

- Customer satisfaction
- Product conformity
- Process- and product-related characteristics and trends
- Supplier

This comprehensive data analysis is designed to verify the suitability and effectiveness of the system and identify potential targets for continual improvement. The second aspect was not part of QS-9000. Note that there is an implied relationship between clauses 8.4 and 5.6, Management review, and clause 8.5.1, Continual improvement. Clause 8.4 states that, "The organization shall determine, collect, and analyze appropriate data to demonstrate the suitability and effectiveness of the quality management system, and to evaluate where continual improvement of the effectiveness of the quality management system can be made."

In other words, the analysis is not to be casual but used for the purpose of demonstrating the effectiveness of the BMS and identifying where continual improvement can be made. The opportunities for continual improvement identified in clause 8.4 must be reviewed by top management. According to clause 5.6, Management review, "The review shall include assessing opportunities for improvement and need for changes…" Furthermore, clause 5.6.2, Review input, requires "recommendations for improvement" as one of the inputs to management review. These opportunities for improvement should be discussed during the review, with the output to include "decisions and actions related to improvement of the effectiveness of the [BMS] and its processes, and improvement of product related to customer requirements…"

Figure 7.2—BMS Control Plan Example

					Example From a BMS Control Plan				
Organization: _____ General Manager: _____					Product Description: _____ Issue/Rev. Date: _____				
Process Activity	Customer Req./Expectation	Key Process & COP	Measurement	Responsibility	Acceptance Criteria 2002	Review frequency	Control Methods	Comments/ Reaction	
					Q1, Q2, Q3, Q4				
				EXAMPLES					
Business fufillment	On-time delivery	K	% On-time in operations	Logistics	95%, 97%, 97%, 100%	Four/year	Monthly management meeting	Corrective action after 3 consecutive	
			% On-time to customer	Production control	100%	Four/year	Trend chart	C/A is more than 15% off target	
Customer complaint	Provide timely response	C	Complaint response	Quality	10 days	100/year	Production control dept.	Continue to monitor	
Design and development	Meet timing requirements		Time to market	Design/dev.	52 weeks 20 per year	Weekly	Quality department	R, Y, G reaction	
Business creation	Innovation		Patent filed	Design		Monthly	Design meeting	Continue to monitor	

Once top management has decided on the improvements to be made and has allocated resources for their accomplishment, then continual improvement in line with clause 8.5.1 can take place. In effect, the continual improvement cycle that begins with clause 8.4 moves to clause 5.6 and concludes with clause 8.5.1, which states, "The organization shall continually improve the effectiveness of the quality management system through the use of... analysis of data... and management review." In other words, the opportunities for improvement identified in the analysis of data are reviewed and researched through management review. This becomes the same improvement monitored in clause 8.5.1.

With the additions ISO/TS 16949 made to ISO 9001:2000, analysis of data is part of an even larger BMS relationship involving customer satisfaction (clause 8.2.1), conformity to product requirements (clauses 7.2.1, 8.2.2.3, 8.2.4, and 8.3), characteristics and trends of processes and products (clauses 4.1, 8.2.3, and 8.2.4), and suppliers (clause 7.4.3.2). Because of this larger relationship, the data to be analyzed must come from many sources. For example, the customer satisfaction data to be analyzed must not consist only of customer perception data, customer score cards, and/or customer dissatisfaction data but must also include the data specified in ISO/TS 16949's clause 8.2.1.1, Customer satisfaction—Supplemental. The data for conformity with ISO/TS 16949's product requirements are gathered during contract review (clause 7.2) and then documented in pre-launch and production control plans. These special characteristics data are probably captured in monthly statistical process control reports. Other characteristics' data are captured nonconforming data. Another source of data required by ISO/TS 16949 is derived from clause 8.2.2.3, Product audit, which requires an organization to "audit products at appropriate stages of production and delivery to verify conformity to all specified requirements..."

Measurement and monitoring of processes related to the organization is required in clauses 4.1 and 8.2.3. Organizations should use their BMS control plans (described earlier) to plan and assign overall responsibilities for the measurement and monitoring of processes.

Except for key processes (e.g., product realization, design and development, or manufacturing) that are monitored by top management, all others are measured locally, by departments. Therefore, the organization must assign responsibility for the analysis of data. This responsibility may be centralized or decentralized, but the result should be information that identifies potential opportunities for improvement.

In effect, clause 8.4 requires an organization to establish data management plans. Your organization needs to determine who will collect the data and to what aggregation level. The aggregation of the data has a direct affect on data analysis. Aggregation levels should correspond to the level of detail required for conducting data analysis. For example, delivery data gathered by the customer would identify how well your organization is meeting customer delivery requirements but would not tell you what products (and which of your departments) were late. If this type of data analysis is required, your organization needs to gather sufficient data by both customer and department, as well as by product, to allow analysis on these levels. Finally, for data management and aggregation, you have to consider where the data are available, who will collect data, who will analyze data, and what type of information is required for problem solving and continual improvement.

Most organizations obtain large savings through the use of good data management plans and automated data collection. Often, a variety of employees already gather the same type of data in several different ways. Worse yet, these data often are not in agreement. If these data can be collected once in an effective and efficient way, made available to everyone who needs it, and acted on by all in the same way, the organization will realize immense savings and real benefits.

So far, this chapter has discussed the ISO 9001:2000 requirements for analysis of data. ISO/TS 16949 also adds clause 8.4.1, Analysis and use of data. This clause is not new; it was present in QS-9000. Clause 8.4.1 adds requirements, as stated in its title, for the use of data. It states that, "Trends in quality and operational performance shall be compared with progress toward objectives and then lead to action…"

Quality and operational performance data can be thought of as measurements related to the product realization process, as required in clauses 4.1; 5.1.1, Process efficiency; and 8.2.3. However, note that clause 8.4.1 requires that this data be compared with progress toward objectives. The overall objectives are to be set by top management (as per clause 5.4.1) and then deployed into the manufacturing plants, where specific quality and operational performance data can be tracked.

Clause 8.4.1 also relates this data analysis to addressing overall customer-related problems and trends. The analyzed operational and quality data need to be compared with "progress toward objectives." This leads to actions for improvement, including the provision of prompt solutions to customer-related problems and the determination of trends affecting the customer. Determining trends must contribute to "status review, decision making, and longer term planning." This identifies issues to be addressed as well as processes and practices that have positive effects and should be maintained and enhanced. Clause 8.4.1 requires linkages between data analysis and customer needs and expectations (as per clause 5.2, Customer focus) as well as customer satisfaction (as per clause 8.2.1). Finally, data analysis relating to the customer also needs to be linked to longer term planning (i.e., clause 5.4.2, Quality management system planning).

It's important to learn from ISO 9001:2000's clause 8.4 and the ISO/TS 16949's clause 8.4.1 that your organization is not only required to collect data but it must also collect data relevant to measuring BMS process effectiveness and customer(s) satisfaction and then act on this data. ISO 9001:1994 required a great deal of documentation, including procedures, which made for a nice paper trail but didn't always lead to improvement and responsiveness to customer needs.

Although QS-9000 was more attuned to the pursuit of improvement and customer satisfaction, ISO/TS 16949 represents a more proactive approach to business/quality management.

Chapter 8

Customer-Specific Requirements, IAOB, and the IATF

Customer-specific requirements are a component of ISO/TS 16949 that cannot be ignored. In fact, customer-specific requirements are more important in ISO/TS 16949 than they were in QS-9000, which considered them as part of the requirements. Furthermore, the customer-specific requirements of DaimlerChrysler, Ford, and GM were the only essential "requirements" in implementing and auditing QS-9000.

ISO/TS 16949 changes this situation. The International Automotive Task Force (IATF), which consists of nine OEMs —six more than the original three that developed QS-9000—used a different strategy to create ISO/TS 16949. When all of the IATF members could not agree on a certain clause or process, the objecting OEM put that particular clause into its own customer-specific requirements. Consequently, there are many more customer core requirements. The five Automotive Industry Action Group (AIAG) reference manuals, which were understood to be core requirements of QS-9000, are now customer-specific requirements of DaimlerChrysler, Ford, and GM.

ISO/TS 16949:1999 introduced a diagram that showed the relationship between ISO 9001:1994, ISO/TS 16949:1999 and customer-specific requirements. (See figure 8.1.)

Figure 8.1 shows that ISO 9001 is considered a base set of requirements that ISO/TS 16949 builds upon for the automotive sector. ISO/TS 16949 tells the supplier to conform to company- (i.e., customer-) specific requirements in addition to ISO/TS 16949's requirements. Additional requirements may include division-specific requirements, commodity-specific requirements, or part-specific requirements. Examples of division-specific requirements include a semiconductor commodity sup-

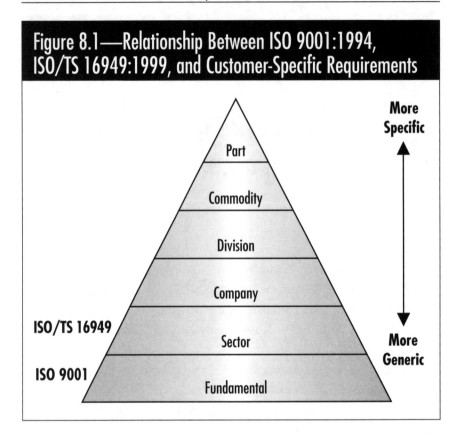

Figure 8.1—Relationship Between ISO 9001:1994, ISO/TS 16949:1999, and Customer-Specific Requirements

plier to a DaimlerChrysler plant, or a heat treat supplier to a Ford Powertrain division. The semiconductor supplier has to contend with the following requirements: ISO 9001:2000; ISO/TS 16949; five reference manuals, which are part of DaimlerChrysler's requirements; semiconductor commodity-specific requirements (formerly called Semiconductor Supplement requirements) issued by the Automotive Electronics Council; and part-specific requirements from a contract review. Similarly, the heat treat supplier to Ford Powertrain has to implement ISO 9001:2000, ISO/TS 16949, five reference manuals, heat treat requirements specific to Ford, a DCP control plan methodology specific to the Ford Powertrain division, and part-specific requirements of that particular heat-treated part, derived from contract review.

Needless to say, the customer-specific requirements have gained a whole new degree of importance in ISO/TS 16949. In fact, customer-specific requirements will be a challenge when implementing and/or auditing ISO/TS 16949. In this chapter, we will discuss the documentation requirements and other strategies for implementing ISO/TS 16949. We will touch on the auditing requirements, briefly covering the key customer-specific requirements of DaimlerChrysler, Ford, and GM.

DOCUMENTATION REQUIREMENTS FOR CUSTOMER-SPECIFIC REQUIREMENTS

Customer-specific documentation requirements are stated in the customer-specific documents of DaimlerChrysler, Ford, and GM. The DaimlerChrysler requirement says, "All ISO/TS 16949 requirements and the requirements of this document (i.e., customer-specific requirements) shall be documented in the organization's quality system." The Ford and GM customer-specific documents say, "All ISO/TS 16949:2002 requirements and the requirements of this document shall be addressed by the organization's quality system." The DaimlerChrysler requirement asks the organization to trace each "shall" to ensure that it has been included in the documented system. The Ford and GM requirements ask the organization and the auditor to ensure that each "shall" has been addressed by the organization's business/quality system. DaimlerChrysler's documentation requirements are more precise and place a greater documentation burden on the organization.

Organizations should map the customer-specific requirements into their process documentation or work instructions. Through this method, both current and future employees can become knowledgeable of customer-specific requirements as they work within a process.

If your organization does not use this strategy, it will have difficulty separating out customer-specific requirements and addressing the issue of how employees are to ensure process repeatability. For example, clause 4.1.6 of the GM customer-specific requirements says, "All design changes, including those proposed by the suppliers, shall have written customer approval, or waiver of such approval, prior to production implementation." This is a detail that needs to be built into the process. It is not possible for a management system to address such a requirement without building it into a process, work instruction, form, or checklist.

CREATING A STRATEGY FOR CUSTOMER-SPECIFIC REQUIREMENTS

The strategy for addressing customer-specific requirements should be as follows: First, the organization must identify and assemble all of the customer-specific requirements from its customer base. This could include Honda, Toyota, GM, Ford,

DaimlerChrysler, Dana, Magna, or Delphi. Second, the organization must create a matrix of all requirements. For example, the organization should use the most comprehensive set of requirements upon which to build the matrix. Among the Big Three, the most comprehensive requirements are in the Ford documents, which can be used to map all of the other customer-specific documents. Finally, once the most comprehensive requirements are identified, the organization must identify the process or work instruction into which to map those requirements. (See figure 8.2.)

With this three-step strategy, the customer-specific requirements can be mapped into your organization's processes. When contract review is performed, this document as well as subsequent processes will need to be updated. Organizations need a process to update customer-specific requirements that is initiated during contract review (sales). Then this process will need to be updated and employees trained as necessary.

Large organizations that have plants which only serve one particular customer don't have to use the most comprehensive matrix, but can simply use that customer's specific requirements. Some interesting questions arise when plants have conflicting requirements. Can common processes be employed in the organization if requirements vary between plants and/or locations? An organization should adopt one process, and indicate in the process that locations supplying one particular customer have to perform certain tasks in a different, and perhaps conflicting, manner. In this way, the process documentation is the same but can be customized for each customer.

DAIMLERCHRYSLER REQUIREMENTS

We have addressed the documentation requirements of ISO/TS 16949. Record-retention requirements from QS-9000 are now found in, and are similar to, DaimlerChrysler, Ford, and GM customer-specific requirements. DaimlerChrysler uses a method called product assurance planning (PAP). This process and/or advance product quality planning (APQP) is used by DaimlerChrysler for product creation. An organization implementing ISO/TS 16949 needs to understand PAP and APQP, and needs to train personnel who interface with DaimlerChrysler for product creation. The DaimlerChrysler requirements detail symbols used for special characteristics (ISO/TS 16949 clause 4.2.1.3 through 4.2.1.5). Both DaimlerChrysler and Ford require annual layouts of product. This requirement should be listed as one of the ongoing controls in the design verification plan (DVP) or in the production con-

Figure 8.2—Sample Audit Matrix

ISO/TS Clause	Ford	GM	DaimlerChrysler	Your Process
4.1	None	None	None	
4.2	1. All ISO/TS and Ford-specific requirements shall be documented	1. All ISO/TS and GM-specific requirements shall be documented	1. All ISO/TS and DaimlerChrysler-specific requirements shall be documented	Add your own company's processes below
4.2.2	4.1 Scope	1. Scope	1. Scope	
4.2.3	4.2	None	None	Document Control
4.2.3.1	4.3 Heat Treat	None	None	
4.2.4	None	None	None	
4.2.4.1	4.4 Retention	4.1.2 Retention	4.1.2 Retention	Records Control
5.1	None	None	None	
5.1.1	None	None	None	
5.2	4.5	None	None	
5.3	None	None	None	
5.4	None	None	None	
5.4.1	None	None	None	
5.4.2	None	None	None	
5.5	None	None	None	
5.5.2.1	4.6 Customer representative	None	None	

trol plan. DaimlerChrysler's requirements conclude with requirements in clause 4.2.1.16, "Forever" requirements—Extended enterprise, and clause 4.2.1.17, Electronic communication. The extended enterprise network requirements are an interface into the organization's change management process (ref. 7.1.4). DaimlerChrysler's electronic communication requirements are defined in the last requirement of its document.

FORD REQUIREMENTS

Ford's requirements are the most comprehensive of the Big Three. This section will highlight the most rigorous and important requirements specified by Ford.

The requirements begin in clause 4.1, with a clear statement of scope—the entire supplier facility (supplying automotive product) to Ford needs to be registered to ISO/TS 16949. Clause 4.3 introduces heat-treating specifications W-HTX for organizations that supply heat-treated products or services. Additionally, Heat Treat Survey Guidelines and Ford Engineering Material specifications WSS-M99A3-A (to reduce risks of embrittlement) are cited. Clause 4.4 cites Ford's record retention requirements, including the requirement to record actual data for variable measurement inspection records.

Clause 4.5 introduces the Q1 requirements and QOS requirements—both Ford systems that require supplier training. Clause 4.7, Management review, requires that a monthly QOS meeting be held, as required by the Q1 manufacturing site assessment. The Ford requirements specify in clause 4.9 that all individuals working on Ford manufacturing and design be trained in appropriate Ford systems. Clause 4.11 requires that implementation plans, as defined in the Ford Lean system requirements, be available. Clause 4.14 defines the Ford Quality and Reliability Requirements and stresses that suppliers follow them. Clause 4.17 states that volume changes greater than 20 percent require that manufacturing feasibility reviews be performed. Requirements for FMEAs, control plans, and special characteristics are detailed in clause 4.20. Clause 4.22 specifies the use of a Ford product development system when reviewing designs. Design verification (clause 4.23) must be performed to vehicle design specifications and system design specifications. Clause 4.25 not only specifies which production part approval process (PPAP) requirements need to be met by tier-two suppliers but also stresses that all tiers' PPAP requirements need to be managed by the supplier. Suppliers need to know the Ford WERS system, SREA, run-at-rate process, and the phased PPAP requirements. Clause 4.27 covers Ford's subcontractor development requirements and includes requirements for second-party assessments. Clause 4.34 specifies that the organization must use the logistics requirements spelled out by the material planning and logistics department, which includes implementation of MS-9000 or material management operation guidelines.

Clause 4.35 indicates that gage repeatability and reproducibility testing needs to be carried out annually on each gage, similar to the Q-101 requirements of the past. Family gage studies are acceptable, but they require approval from the supplier technical assistance (STA) department. The organization must monitor performance and customer satisfaction metrics defined in Q1, and the Ford SIM requirements must be reviewed twice weekly, as per clause 4.38. Ford and GM have detailed requirements for internal auditors, as referenced in clause 4.39. Clause 4.40 requires that all process controls have a goal of variation reduction using Six Sigma or some other method. Clause 4.43 specifies that appearance items or characteristics that can be seen by the customer must conform to Ford global craftsmanship requirements. Clause 4.44 says that customer concerns regarding containment and root cause analysis must be completed in five days and an 8-D must be completed in ten business days.

The Ford requirements mention that suppliers need to understand and apply the following systems, methodologies, and processes: Ford W-HTX, Ford Heat Treating Survey Guidelines, Engineering Material specifications WSS-M99 A3-A, QOS, Q1, Manufacturing Site Assessment, Ford Lean System Requirements, Ford Quality and Reliability Requirements, FPDS, VDS, SDS, PPAP and Phased PPAP, MSA, WERS, SREA, Run at Rate, MMOG, MS-9000, Six Sigma, and 8-D.

GM REQUIREMENTS

The GM requirements are not as comprehensive as Ford's requirements. GM requirement 4.1.5 cites special characteristics (i.e., key characteristic designations) specified by GM. Clause 4.1.8 specifies the use of the PPAP manual by suppliers, and that suppliers must compare business/quality system performance and customer satisfaction metrics with those of competitors, or with an appropriate benchmark (4.1.9). Internal auditor qualifications are quite detailed and are similar to Ford's. Clauses 4.1.10 through 4.1.11.3 detail requirements for internal auditors, supplier quality management system development, second-party audit approval criteria, and supplier development for small suppliers. Clause 4.2.2 specifies fifteen GM-specific documents that must be used by suppliers, including KCDS, pre-prototype and prototype, continual improvement procedure, run at rate, etc. GM also defines a deadline for achieving ISO/TS 16949 registration and specifies that QS-9000 expires on December 14, 2006.

IMPLEMENTING CUSTOMER-SPECIFIC REQUIREMENTS

As mentioned previously, implementation begins with training. Key supplier personnel must be trained in customer-specific requirements. Customer requirements typically come in two levels of specificity: identifying how a process should operate, or requiring an entirely new process or method.

Detailed customer specifics can be implemented into processes by following a documentation strategy. Mapping the customer-specific requirements to processes is the least risky, and so the best, documentation strategy. Adopt a common process for the entire organization and clearly indicate different ways tasks should be performed to satisfy different customers.

Organizations should follow these steps when adopting customer-specific requirements:

1. Adopt the most stringent requirement.
2. Describe how tasks may be different for different customers.
3. Add different forms for different customers if the submission methods differ.
4. Measure processes differently if customer measurement criteria vary.

Some customer criteria cannot be implemented just by mapping them into existing processes. Customer specifics may ask suppliers to adopt a certain system. For example, DaimlerChrysler requires the use of Powerway, and Ford requires the use of a particular CAD system. Sometimes, the requirements mandate an entire implementation (e.g., MS-9000 or MMOG (by Ford) or Ford Q1 requirements). Teams must be formed for these specific implementations and the mandates must be completed as a part of ISO/TS 16949 implementation.

AUDITING REQUIREMENTS FOR CUSTOMER-SPECIFIC REQUIREMENTS

Utilizing document review is the best method for determining whether the organization has already considered all of the customer-specific requirements. The internal auditor needs to have a detailed document review checklist with the "shalls" clearly delineated. The organization must complete the checklist, showing where it believes the customer-specific requirements are documented. The auditor will check to see if the processes indeed demonstrate evidence of compliance with the customer-specific requirements. As mentioned previously, some requirements are processes that would only be audited during an onsite audit.

Once the auditor has checked each process and ensured that the processes demonstrate evidence of compliance with the customer's specifics, then the requirements can be discarded and the process documentation used for the on-site audit. Trying to audit customer-specific requirements during an onsite audit without the document review is difficult and time-consuming.

Chapter 9

Documenting ISO/TS 16949:2002

SO/TS 16949:2002's structure is based on five principal components, not the twenty clauses of ISO 9001:1994. This new structure is not simply a rearrangement of twenty clauses into five components. It involves a significant reorganization that brings together requirements from different elements, divides up those requirements, and spreads them throughout the five sections.

For an organization with a QS-9000-based business/quality management system (BMS), the new structure is not simply a matter of regrouping procedures or putting a matrix in front of the procedures manual.

The intent of ISO/TS 16949 is to streamline organizational processes, avoid the previous compartmentalization of business/quality system requirements, and establish the cross-functional nature of a BMS. This fundamental change will significantly affect the documentation structure of an organization's BMS. The process characteristics and the turtle analysis are de facto methods for process documentation. Although ISO 9001:2000 provides greater flexibility regarding the need for documented procedures and documentation, ISO/TS 16949 will reestablish some of the documentation requirements from QS-9000 to suit automotive OEM needs.

This need to document more than ISO 9001:2000's six documented procedures is evident in the customer-specific requirements. GM and Ford state that all "ISO/TS 16949:2002 requirements and the requirements of this document shall be addressed by the organization's quality system, and the customer-specific requirements need to be documented." DaimlerChrysler's customer-specific requirements substitute the word "documented" with "addressed."

At a minimum, the traditional policy-based business/quality manual will need to be rewritten and reoriented. Key changes to ISO/TS 16949 are likely to involve the process mapping and process orientation required by ISO 9001:2000.

Organizations that have structured their procedures to mimic the QS-9000 elements can expect to do some major document rework. ISO/TS 16949 requires companies to document their product realization process (i.e., the process of creating and producing new products, from concept to delivery to the customer).

This process has a larger scope than the current advanced product quality planning (APQP) process and may require organizations to start with the very act of product idea formation, or the "product concept," and end with product shipping. Also, as stated in chapter 3, the customer-oriented processes (COPs) need to be identified and documented. Support-oriented processes (SOPs) that affect the capability of the product realization process (e.g., procurement and staffing), and management-oriented processes (MOPs) (e.g., internal audit, corrective and preventive action, and document control) and business processes (e.g., marketing and advertising) will need to be identified, as shown in figure 9.1

The process map in figure 9.1 is an example of what a manufacturing organization can develop to show the sequence and interaction of its processes. This is a requirement of clauses 4.1b, Quality management system—General requirements, and 4.2.2c Documentation requirements—Quality manual.

Such a map is helpful in understanding how the processes in an organization interconnect. An organization implementing ISO/TS 16949 will need to re-orient its documentation and the BMS to understand that its business is a series of interrelated processes. This can be seen as a culture change within a company—breaking down the walls of the hierarchical organization and gaining an understanding of the cross-functional nature of the business.

DOCUMENTING PROCESSES

Even though documenting all these processes is not required by ISO 9001:2000, the customer-specific requirements and process characteristics require processes to be documented according to ISO/TS 16949. Additionally, even ISO 9001:2000 requires evidence that "ensures the effective planning, operation, and control of its processes" (4.2.1b, Documentation requirements—General). Organizations must also "ensure the availability of resources and information necessary to support the operation and monitoring of these processes" (4.1d, Quality management system—

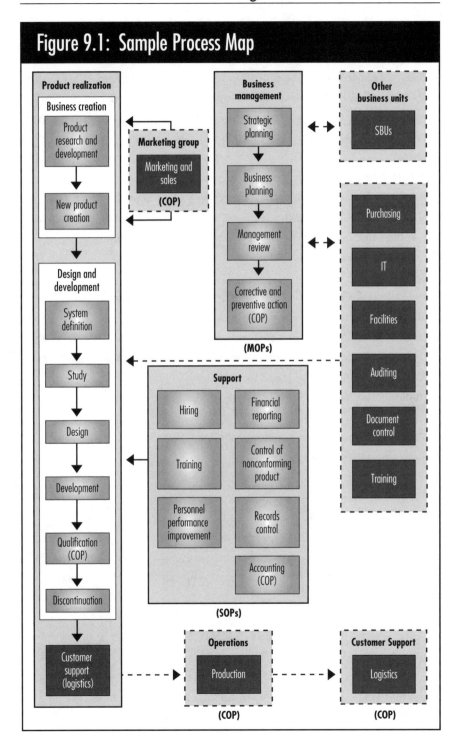

Figure 9.1: Sample Process Map

General requirements). Clause 4.1e also requires that all processes be measured, monitored, and improved.

This is a major new expectation, even for organizations registered to QS-9000 or ISO/TS 16949:1999. Your organization should consider using process flows to document nonmanufacturing processes. Process flows can also be used to effectively document a process and serve as its written procedures, as shown in the example in figure 9.2.

Figure 9.2 shows a sample procedure that documents a process for corrective and preventive action. The flowchart shows each step of the process, who is responsible, and specific notes on each step. Each step of the process can be investigated for problems or improvements using process failure mode and effects analysis (PFMEA) or an action plan.

CONDUCTING PROCESS ANALYSIS

Before creating the process flow of an organization's process, it's best to use process analysis or turtle diagramming. This method allows the team to study the process analytically to understand resource needs, competency requirements, measurement and monitoring, and standards and methods used in the process. The author uses the turtle analysis and a process chart designer that captures process characteristics described in chapter 3, pages 44-45.

Process documentation requirements used by the author involve:

■ Process analysis (turtle)
■ Process chart designer (process characteristics)
■ Process flow

The measurements used for process measurement must be documented and included in the BMS control plan. Automotive companies should employ BMS control plans immediately as effective ways to enhance competitive capability and improve the bottom line.

WORK INSTRUCTIONS

The work instructions for ISO/TS 16949 do not require any additional rework when compared to QS-9000. Work instructions in QS-9000 were predominantly driven by clause 4.9.1, Process monitoring and operator instructions. The compa-

Figure 9.2—Sample Procedure

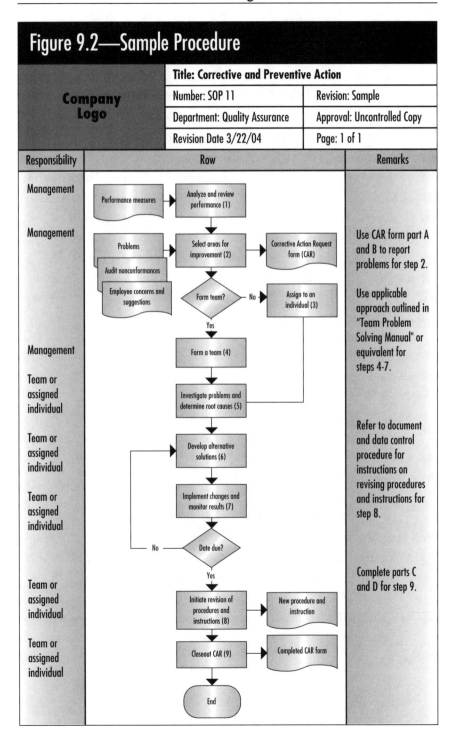

rable requirements in ISO/TS 16949 (clause 7.5) are much less demanding. This is an opportunity for organizations to lighten the paperwork at operator workstations.

STRATEGY FOR DOCUMENTATION

There is a great need for companywide standardization of documentation. Most companies with multiple sites and plants should have one business/quality manual (level one), common and site-specific procedures (level two), and common and site-specific work instructions (level three). Processes like purchasing, sales, internal audits, and management review are also common. Some procedures that are site- or customer-specific cannot be standardized and so must be plant- or site-specific. The forms and checklists (level four) are the methods used by organizations to record work. These should also have common and specific layers. The decision to standardize documentation is a top management decision. To accomplish standardization, top management must use its muscle for implementation purposes. (See figure 9.3.)

In large organizations serving multiple customers, how should quality systems be designed? Should they be stand alone or integrated? A stand-alone system is easier to implement but provides inconsistent processes and doesn't present the same "face" to the customer at different sites. Integrated systems are consistent but need to be designed with flexibility, strict rules, and governance.

Most organizations that adopt common procedures on level one and two experience an unintended consequence—the creation of many and varied work instructions. This is one of the pitfalls organizations need to be careful about.

MULTISITE ORGANIZATION

Organizations have processes that connect multiple sites. For example, a customer product inquiry that results in a quote may start at sales, travel to design, go on to the manufacturing plant, and finally end up with top management for a sign-off. Even with ISO 9001:2000 and ISO/TS 16949 in place, it's difficult to document processes that show how the entire organization works. These interfaces between organizations or sites are another opportunity for organizational effectiveness and process efficiency.

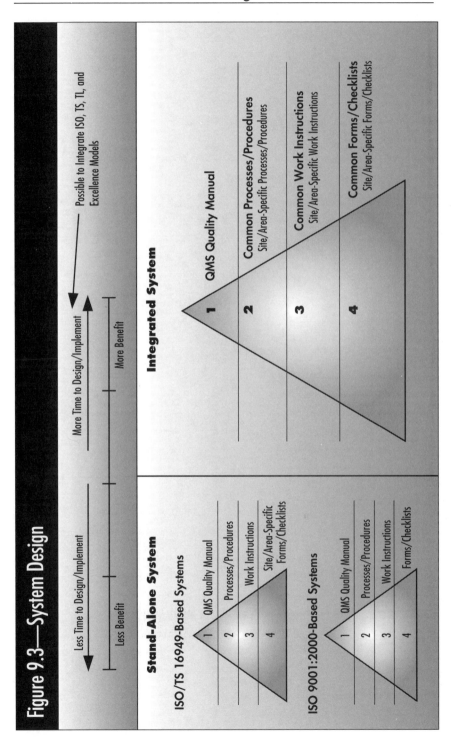

Figure 9.3—System Design

Chapter 10

Transitioning From QS-9000 to ISO/TS 16949:2002

What is the future of automotive sector-specific quality management system (QMS) requirements? (Remember, think of your QMS as a business management system [BMS].)As the book goes to press, it's evident that some organizations are taking the compliance approach to implementing ISO/TS 16949:2002—using process maps that identify QS-9000 procedures as processes—without too much top management involvement. This lack of top management involvement makes the transition from QS-9000 to ISO/TS 16949 nothing but a documentation shuffle that will result in major nonconformances.

This chapter will discuss how involving top management is essential to a successful transition from QS-9000 to ISO/TS 16949. It will also present six steps your organization can take to prepare for the future.

1. CREATE A PROCESS MAP AND UNDERSTAND CUSTOMER REQUIREMENTS

Before you do anything, study your organization—follow the product-development process and interview personnel involved in that process. To create a process map, you must identify all of your organization's key activities, from new product ideation to research, and on to design and development, production, all the way through to shipping and delivery procedures. Identify the customer-oriented processes (COPs) in your organization. What are the customer inputs and outputs? To ensure that your final process map is useful to your organization, identify all the management-oriented processes (MOPs) and support-oriented processes (SOPs). (See chapter 3 for a more detailed discussion of the process approach.) The key to understanding your processes is to interview departments regarding their activities and to create a process map by working backward.

Next, determine who your customers are. Decide whether the BMS you create will support only customers or if it will also satisfy the requirements of all the interested parties for your organization.

The implications of this decision are immense. The processes needed to support interested parties (e.g., owners/investors, lenders, personnel, suppliers/partners, and the community) may result in incorporating many more processes to your process map.

ISO 9004:2000's clause 5.2, Customer focus—Needs and expectations of interested parties, contains useful guidance and recommendations on this topic. It's important to understand each need and expectation of your customers and/or interested parties. Such understanding will help answer the question of what process or set of processes will satisfy those expectations. Your organization may find that it actually needs to create new processes.

Finally, check to see whether the process map includes all ISO/TS 16949 processes. Do you have processes for clause 7.2.3, Customer communication, and/or process for clause 5.5.3, Internal communications? Are there processes for capturing and analyzing customer expectations for product (i.e., customer requirements as envisioned in clause 7.2.1, Determination of requirements related to the product)?

It's important to determine the scope of your implementation. What organizations and what processes are included? How will the processes link with each other? How will the site and remote location link with each other?

2. CONDUCT A GAP ANALYSIS OF THE EXISTING SYSTEM

Examine the documentation structure behind your organization's BMS. Have you documented the necessary processes? Use the process map created in step 1 to identify the process documentation you have currently. Complete the process list in chapter 3, figure 3.8. What processes need to be documented still?

Remember Chapter 8? Are all the requirements (i.e., "shalls") of ISO/TS 16949:2002 and customer specific requirements documented? Chapter 8 recommended documenting all "requirements." Next, identify if you would like to re-document some of your QS-9000 procedures as a process flow. If so, verify whether you have "documents needed by the organization to ensure the effective planning, operation, and control of its processes," as required by clause 4.2.1.d, Documentation requirements—General. Also, determine if "both the operation and control of these processes are effective," as per clause 4.1.c, Quality management system—General requirements.

Taking these steps involves asking questions about the existing BMS and your customers' specific requirements regarding documentation. This step should result in the clarification of your organization's documentation needs for satisfying customers and/or interested parties. ISO 9001:2000 does not restrict an organization from documenting any process that is part of its BMS, but it does require six procedures to be documented that were already required by QS-9000 and ISO/TS 16949:1999. Ultimately, the International Automotive Task Force (IATF) has retained documentation requirements in ISO/TS 16949:2002 beyond those required by ISO 9001:2000. (See chapter 9.) Once you have taken the steps outlined here, you must conduct an audit or gap analysis to prepare your organization to revise its QS-9000-registered business/quality system to conform to ISO/TS 16949.

Using ISO/TS 16949, the gaps between your organization and ISO/TS 16949's requirements can be identified. Appendix A lays out the key differences of this transition to show you where you need to focus. Also, the previous chapters provide guidance on each of these key differences.

Focusing solely on compliance will do your organization a great disservice. Study your organizational needs. What key indicators and what processes need improvement? Are your new product launches habitually late? Are customers dissatisfied with your lead time? Identify these organizational gaps. Also ask questions about the supply base and your management system.

The automotive industry is undergoing structural changes. The last twenty years heralded the emergence of automotive suppliers and markets in Southeast Asia. This next decade will see the emergence of China and India as key markets and as a supply source of automotive parts. The supply chain and the internal network of plants will become even more global. There will be greater pressure for higher quality and lower costs. OEMs will be forced to develop a greater variety of products to meet customer needs.

There are the nine changes that need to be considered when designing business/quality systems in accordance with ISO/TS 16949. Each of the nine initiatives shown below can result in savings for your organization.

Paradigm Shift in Quality Expectations

U.S. OEMs have made a paradigm shift in their quality expectations. What was considered good ten years ago is no longer acceptable. Customers no longer accept shipments with a few bad products. Even if your overall ppm is low (<60), you may have a problem. These new quality expectations require suppliers to have much better internal systems than previously sufficed.

Outsourcing and the Extended Supply Chain

U.S. automotive manufacturers will soon be forced to extend their supply chain of products and services to China and India. This change will also affect internal processes. Supply chain processes such as supplier development, manufacturing, technology transfer, and information management will all be affected. Outsourcing is an option that by itself will create significant savings and is the U.S. automotive industry's only choice for survival in the new global economy

New Product Development

Most tier-one supplier design processes are cumbersome and time-consuming. Designing nimble processes that reduce product launch risk, reduce lead time, and provide for Six Sigma product quality is essential for the future. This initiative, in conjunction with cost of quality (below), can create major savings for the organization. Product design cost savings are a major source of savings for most organizations.

Strategic Planning Systems

As discussed earlier, the coming decade will present many challenges to manufacturers. Key questions for management include:

- What products should the organization keep and what products should be abandoned?
- How can the organization reduce costs 20 to 30 percent to keep customers?
- How often does the organization meet to discuss present trends and activities?
- Does the organization's strategic planning allow for strategic and team decision making?
- Are these types of discussions taking place between corporate top management, purchasing, sales, and plant management? Note that this is a management and process problem.

Redefining Cost of Quality

Cost of quality (COQ) systems must be updated to new models that allow for true recognition of areas that need attention. Companies like Intel and IBM are using new COQ models to generate millions of dollars of improvement savings. The key to redefining COQ is the rule of first-pass success. In product quality, this results in rework and scrap, but the rule can be used for any process.

Implementation of Lean and Six Sigma Initiatives

Is the company using Lean/Six Sigma Black Belts to reduce internal waste? Each Black Belt working with Green and Yellow Belts can save the average company more than $1 million a year. How many Black Belts do you have? Does your organization support this process? Have you redefined your management system to incorporate Lean/Six Sigma?

Integration of Business Management Systems

When implementing ISO/TS 16949, organizations must attempt to merge all of their practices (including environmental, safety, Six Sigma, and Lean) into one business management system (BMS). Not only will this pay dividends in terms of internal and external auditing, but it will also produce real benefits by teaching internal staff that the processes they need to follow are defined in one documented system.

Linkage of Processes

When designing processes in ISO/TS 16949, there is the opportunity to link processes between the plant, design, corporate, sales, and purchasing. Current practice does not allow this. Each of the entities within an organization has designed processes that start and end within their four walls. Refining and redesigning processes for the enterprise as a whole will allow organizational entities to work more quickly and efficiently, and eliminate waste.

Implementing Enterprisewide Quality Software

Enterprisewide quality software is one of the most important movements within industry today. The linkages between plants and design centers for new-product development, performance metrics, project management, continual improvement, customer expectations, and human resources that an enterprisewide quality software system can afford are imperative to the success of an organization.

Once the gaps have been identified, your organization should develop a timing plan for implementing ISO/TS 16949, which requires two methodologies. The first links customer expectations to objectives and then to key processes; this is called the business operating system (BOS) process. The second institutionalizes continual improvement at the process level and is called the process review methodology (PRM).

3. GETTING TOP MANAGEMENT INVOLVEMENT

Top management involvement is essential to the successful implementation of ISO/TS 16949. About 33 percent of auditors' time will be spent auditing top management. Remember that ISO/TS 16949 is concerned with the effectiveness of the organization. It only makes sense that top management should be involved.

Management involvement in the process focus and customer focus is vital to the organization's success. Also, the process map and process metrics documented in the BMS control plan must be discussed by the management team in the management meetings.

Finally, management must view ISO/TS 16949 implementation as an improvement process rather than a compliance issue. Adopting the nine initiatives described in the previous section and demonstrating dollar savings as a result of ISO/TS 16949 implementation is essential to obtaining top management support.

4. BECOMING PROCESS-FOCUSED

Process review methodology (PRM) concerns documenting and controlling BMS processes. It applies turtle diagrams, process flows, and BMS control plans to processes in the process map and to your organization's documentation to ensure your organization's documentation is effective and that its BMS processes are under control. (See chapters 3 and 9 for more details.)

Each process owner needs to measure the process and show improvement in it. It's helpful to use a failure mode and effects analysis or action plans to document improvement, as required by clauses 4.1.f and 8.2.3. A BMS control plan is used at the process level for planning the types of controls required to ensure that the actual output of the process meets the intended outcome. This document links the BOS process measurables with the PRM approach.

Figure 10.1—Process Review Methodology

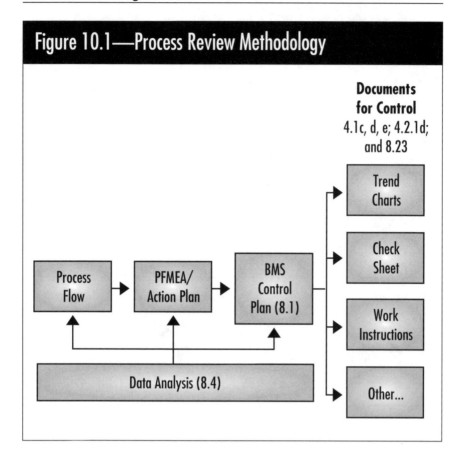

These tools also work well in nonmanufacturing settings. QS-9000-registered organizations are using PRM (as displayed in figure 10.1) to document, control, and improve their nonmanufacturing processes. This author recommends the following for process documentation: process analysis (turtle), process chart designer, and process flow.

Finally, don't forget the four tools to become process-focused: process maps, process lists, BMS control plans, and alignment charts. (See chapters 3 and 4 for more details.)

5. IMPLEMENT CUSTOMER FOCUS

The first step in becoming customer focused involves identifying customer and interested party expectations. (See chapter 4.) One method is to use a process that lists, groups, and rates expectations using Post-it notes. By grouping these customer

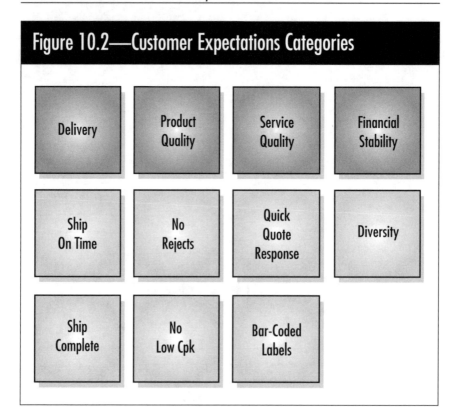

Figure 10.2—Customer Expectations Categories

Delivery	Product Quality	Service Quality	Financial Stability
Ship On Time	No Rejects	Quick Quote Response	Diversity
Ship Complete	No Low Cpk	Bar-Coded Labels	

expectations into categories, it's easier to align the customers' or interested parties' expectations with processes and metrics, as demonstrated in figure 10.2.

Another key step in this methodology is the use of alignment charts to link each expectation category to the key processes and process measurables that need to be measured and monitored to satisfy the requirements of clauses 4.1.e and 8.2.3, Monitoring and measurement of processes. Figure 10.3 provides an example of an alignment chart an automotive supplier could use to satisfy critical value-adding requirements of ISO/TS 16949 and to improve both the effectiveness of the BMS and customer satisfaction with the organization.

To effectively satisfy ISO 9001:2000's clause 5.4.1, Planning—Quality objectives, an organization must use benchmarking to determine what its short- and long-term objectives should be. The organization's improvement plans (as per clause 5.4.2, Quality management system planning) can be accomplished by using the BOS. The organization will then be on its way to achieving both enterprise improvement and breakthrough process improvement.

Figure 10.3—Alignment Chart

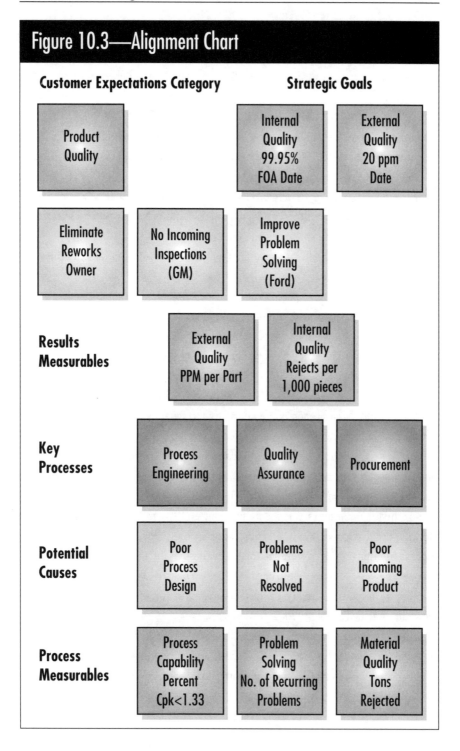

Customer Expectations Category

Strategic Goals

Product Quality

Internal Quality 99.95% FOA Date

External Quality 20 ppm Date

Eliminate Reworks Owner

No Incoming Inspections (GM)

Improve Problem Solving (Ford)

Results Measurables

External Quality PPM per Part

Internal Quality Rejects per 1,000 pieces

Key Processes

Process Engineering

Quality Assurance

Procurement

Potential Causes

Poor Process Design

Problems Not Resolved

Poor Incoming Product

Process Measurables

Process Capability Percent Cpk<1.33

Problem Solving No. of Recurring Problems

Material Quality Tons Rejected

See chapter 4 for a discussion of customer focus. Chapter 4 describes customer focus as implementing the following: customer-focused process, customer expectations matrix, BMS control plan and alignment chart, and a process list.

6. IMPLEMENT ISO/TS 16949

One of the greatest challenges—and benefits—of implementing ISO/TS 16949 is that it requires a QS-9000-registered organization to become customer-focused as well as process-focused.

The other major changes between ISO 9001:1994 and ISO 9001:2000 are shown in appendix A. Also, the steps in documentation and processes were identified in the gap analysis when processes were documented in step 4.

Becoming customer-focused requires an organization to implement a methodology like the customer focus process described in step 5, whereas becoming process-focused requires a process map and an implementation process like PRM. However, process focus also requires an organizational culture change. The application of cross-functional management, matrix organizations, and process-based organizational requirements may be considered but are not required by ISO/TS 16949.

AN ALTERNATIVE: THE MINIMALIST APPROACH

The minimalist approach is the alternative to what clearly is a commitment of resources and involvement of management toward the improvement of the organization. This approach (making no significant change) is one some organizations may opt to take. With this approach, an organization makes changes only to the business/quality manual (level one), by rewriting it to include the BMS's scope and any exclusions claimed by the organization, and by adding a process map that shows a description of the interaction between the procedures of the BMS. This process map would also reference the procedures in the procedures manual (level two). No new procedures would need to be added because typically a QS-9000-conforming system will already have documentation for the seven procedures, as required by ISO/TS 16949:2002.

If the minimalist approach is taken, an organization will need to consider:

■ Is the documentation written around the organization's processes? In other words, the procedures manual must not be written to the elements of QS-9000, but around the organization's business processes.

- Are all the processes required to meet "customer and applicable regulatory requirements" (clause 1.2, Scope—Application) identified within the process map (clause 4.1.a)? Has the organization identified all the processes it needs to satisfy all customer and regulatory needs and expectations?
- If the process map shows that the contract review process flows into the program management process in advanced product quality planning, then the contract review procedure needs to clearly show how it flows to the program management procedure. Is this the case? The inputs and outputs between the two processes need to be carefully defined. This type of linkage must be evident between all processes linked in the process map.
- Are the COPs, MOPs, SOPs and other ISO/TS 16949:2002 requirements documented?
- Is each process, including training and management review, monitored, measured, and analyzed, as per the requirements of clause 4.1.e? Are the process characteristics clear (e.g., a process owner exists, the process is defined, the process is documented, process linkages are established, the process is monitored and improved, records are maintained).

Organizations and auditors need to be careful not to fall into the trap of the minimalist approach. No improvement will be evident in such a "revised" system. More important, the organization will not make any movement toward becoming customer- or process-focused, which is detrimental in the long term, even if the OEMs it supplies never require ISO/TS 16949 registration.

CONCLUSION

A lot of value can be added when ISO/TS 16949:2002 is implemented. Quality organizations need to use this opportunity to not only make the organization comply with ISO/TS 16949:2002 but make the organization more competitive as well. As mentioned in the preface, the key message of the book is the need for acquiring value from the ISO/TS 16949:2002 implementation. At a minimum, ISO/TS 16949:2002 will make organizations both process- and customer-focused. With a little visionary linking, the business/quality system can be used to support the business strategy. This is essential and relevant to the quality-focused organization.

The Seventeen Key ISO/TS 16949:2002 Transition Challenges for QS-9000-Registered Organizations

The table on the following pages shows the 17 key transition challenges QS-9000-registered organizations face when transitioning to ISO/TS 16949.

The Seventeen Key ISO/TS 16949:2002 Transition Challenges for QS-9000-Registered Organizations

Clause/Subclause	Influenced by	Challenges	Chapter Reference
4.1 Quality management system—General requirements	ISO 9001:2000	Requirements for process map (or equivalent), process management, customer-oriented processes, support processes, and process characteristics	3
4.2 Documentation requirements	ISO 9001:2000 and New	Document processes and their interface. Document COPs, MOPs, and SOPs	Scope 3 & 9
5.2 Management responsibility— Customer focus	ISO 9001:2000	Decision on customer vs. interested parties. Need for process to gather "needs and expectations" of customers/interested parties	4
5.4.1 Planning— Quality objectives	ISO 9001:2000 and ISO/TS 16949:1999	Deployed objectives address-ing customer expectations	4
5.5 Internal communication	ISO 9001:2000	Creation of internal commu-nication processes suitable to organization	6
5.6 Management review	ISO 9001:2000 and ISO/TS 16949:1999	Revision of previous manage-ment review process. ISO/TS 16949:2002 adds additional items to be reviewed.	4
6.1 Resource management— Provision of resources	ISO 9001:2000	Establishment of resource allocation process	6

The Seventeen Key ISO/TS 16949:2002 Transition Challenges for QS-9000-Registered Organizations

Clause/Subclause	Influenced by	Challenges	Chapter Reference
6.2 Human resources (particularly 6.2.2.3 and 6.2.2.4)	ISO 9001:2000 and ISO/TS 16949:1999	Provision of job competency, on-the-job training, and employee motivation and empowerment	6
7. Product realization	ISO 9001:2000	Documents for "effective control" of all processes in process map	9
7.1.4 Change control	New	Minor change for most suppliers	7
7.2 Customer-specific requirements	QS-9000	Additional requirements for suppliers are included in the customer-specific requirements, especially Ford.	8
7.3 Design and development	New	Inclusion of design and development of processes, not just product (note required development and use of FMEAs)	5
7.4 Purchasing	New	Inclusion of service suppliers in coverage and use of suppliers monitored indicators. ISO 9001:2000 registration of suppliers	5

The Seventeen Key ISO/TS 16949:2002 Transition Challenges for QS-9000-Registered Organizations

Clause/Subclause	Influenced by	Challenges	Chapter Reference
8.2.1 Monitoring and measurement—Customer satisfaction	ISO 9001:2000	Customer rating for quality and delivery insufficient: monitoring of "customer perceptions" of quality. Importance of customer satisfaction—supplemental requirements, including delivered part quality and schedule performance to IATF	4
8.2.2 Internal Audit	ISO/TS 16949:1999	Manufacturing process and product audits based on COPs and process approach	7
8.2.3 Monitoring and measurement of processes	ISO 9001:2000 and ISO/TS 16949:1999	Process studies on manufacturing processes. Measurement of all processes is process map	7
8.4 Analysis of data	ISO 9001:2000	Increased scope from QS-9000	7